BEAUTIFUL
XIANGXI

BEAUTIFUL XIANGXI

*A Photographic Journey of Hunan
through the Pen of Shen Congwen*

PHOTOGRAPHS BY Zhuo Ya

Reader's
Digest

The Reader's Digest Association, Inc.
Pleasantville, New York / Hong Kong

Chinese edition © 2004 Shanghai Literature & Art Publishing House
English edition © 2004 Shanghai Literature & Art Publishing House and Shanghai Press & Publishing
Development Company

The Reader's Digest Association, Inc. is the authorized publisher of the English edition outside China.

Reader's Digest is a registered trademark of The Reader's Digest Association, Inc.

Project Editors: Susan Randol, Longgen Chen
Project Designers: Yiping Yang, Naiqing Xu, Zongpei Jia
Interior and Cover Design: Yinchang Yuan
Interior and Cover Design Consultant: Nick Anderson
Senior Designer: George McKeon
Executive Editors: Ying Wu, Dolores York
Associate Publisher, Trade Publishing: Christopher T. Reggio
Vice President & Publisher, Trade Publishing: Harold Clarke

Text by Shen Congwen
Photographs by Zhuo Ya

Translation by Mark Kitto

Library of Congress Cataloging in Publication Data
Library of Congress cataloging information has been applied for.
ISBN 0-7621-0638-7

Address any comments about *Beautiful Xiangxi* to:
The Reader's Digest Association, Inc.
Adult Trade Publishing
Reader's Digest Road
Pleasantville, NY 10570-7000

TRANSLATOR'S NOTE
The excerpts that accompany the photographs in this book have been taken from a wide selection of Shen Congwen's writings. Since the time to complete this assignment did not allow for translating all of Shen Congwen's writings, I may not have included all of the nuances and hidden meanings in his writing. My apologies. Should a reader who is more familiar with Shen Congwen's stories and writings uncover a passage where I have missed the point, please forgive me.

rd.com For more Reader's Digest products and information, visit our website.

Printed in China

1 3 5 7 9 10 8 6 4 2

Shen Congwen's Xiangxi

Since 1981 I have sought,
through my camera lens,
the fine portrait of Xiangxi
painted by your pen.

—Zhuo Ya

C
O
N
T
E
N
T
S

别那么镶金镂玉 爱沈从文 光耀和福祉

得朴素一点，像沈从文一样

这将是一本不平常的画册和影集 我倒是有个希望 光耀和福祉 像传说是个

的作品让后几代的乐队指挥演释一样 作曲家得以蒙受像传说是个

这是一种对沈从文作品的重要的演释 令中就好像作曲家紧紧咬住不

个晚上我拆开来看了住连眉毛都差点睏脱了，竟然是这很多年以前

和聪明起来 夹甚至会培养力欣赏力 写对比哈精致

婉约，浓密淡远，发明了对风景的一种从未有过的认 爱沈从文

看起来多美。读起来多么神往 写对比哈精致不

而且是诗 我在湘西上家湘西苗族百治州的

且应该是情感的产物；不仅仅是小说，而且是诗。永远都是 像传说是从湘西

提点出新的想象。光耀和福祉。

苦心了下的湘西地方作一些令天的社会调查，会是件值得做的

INTRODUCTION

Many years ago, while I was at Jishou University in Xiangxi—the local name given to the western part of Hunan Province—I discussed with colleagues how we could compare the Xiangxi of novelist Shen Congwen's time and place and the Xiangxi of today. I thought it was a project worth doing. Everyone nodded in agreement. A comparison of literature and history can provoke new thoughts about each discipline. Like a fish chasing the tail of a fish in front of it, history and literature will always pursue each other through time.

Xiangxi has always frustrated the poets of China. But not Shen Congwen. He describes Xiangxi with the aid of long personal experience. He uses this intimacy to describe the landscape, the vast spaces, the rhythms of life, and the comparisons and contradictions within it. His deeply moving descriptions are both beautiful to read and touching to hear. Readers of Shen Congwen learn from him. They are enriched. They hold their heads higher having read him.

However, readers must go beyond the works of Shen Congwen to fully appreciate the man, to admire his Xiangxi. His books are not just another piece of literature; they are a labor of love. They are not merely novels; they are poetry.

When Zhuo Ya sent me a pile of photographs, I put them aside and thought nothing of them. Then, one evening, I happened to glance through them. I was astounded. My heart missed a beat.

Like the musical notes of a composer's score, these photographs provide an insight into Shen Congwen's literary legacy. These photos will illuminate and enrich generations of readers.

I have high hopes for this unique volume of images. It shouldn't be dressed up or made into a fancy art book. It should be simple, like Shen Congwen himself. Otherwise, I fear he will look down from heaven and laugh.

Huang Yongyu

Huang Yongyu (1924–) is one of China's most famous cultural figures of the last half-century. A renowned artist from Hunan, Yongyu suffered during the Cultural Revolution, went to stay in Hong Kong in the early 1990s, and returned to live in Bejing in 1998.

沈从文 和他的 湘西

I take up this pen because I want to record something of the twenty years I spent in a certain part of the world. I want to describe the people, the sounds, the smells of the place. This was the classroom where I learned all my lessons about life. To start with, though, I must decide how best to describe the remote and distant town that I come from. As they say at home, it really is a very peculiar place.

You will never have heard of any bandits from this area. The local soldiers were as pure at heart as the local peasants. They did not harass or bully anyone. The peasants themselves were brave and peace loving. Moreover, everyone respected the gods and the law. The local merchants dealt in cloth and other everyday items. They wandered freely, deep into the mountains to distant villages where they would barter with the local inhabitants and hope to profit. The hierarchy of the area was divided into several layers. At the top were the celestial spirits. Next were the officials and then below them the head men of the villages and the shamanistic priests who served the spirits. Everyone entrusted their well-being to the

CHAPTER ONE

MY BIRTHPLACE

gods and accepted the law as dispensed by the officials. At least one man in every family was a member of the militia. This entitled his family to go to the barracks and draw a monthly stipend in silver and a measure of rice. It also permitted them to plough and sow on the commons that were appropriated by the government some two hundred years ago.

· · · · · · · · · · · · · · · This is the small town where I was born and spent my first fifteen years. Apart from returning two-and-a-half years after I first left, I have never stepped back through the town gate. Not yet at any rate. But I am intimately familiar with the place. There are still many people living inside those city walls, and I frequently return to my memories of living there with them.

· · · · · · · The mystery of Xiangxi is closely connected with the peculiar character of its people. It could only be in these surroundings that the fantasies of the ancient Chu people could be born and could develop into the moving "Songs of the South." To preserve the heritage of these songs, you need to preserve their birthplace.

Note: "Songs of the South" is a collection of folk songs and poems by many authors, predominant among whom was Qu Yuan. They were collected and published in the Chu Dynasty (400 BC).

Whenever they have the chance, travelers and merchants going upstream follow the route taken by Qu Yuan along the ever-sparkling waters of the Yuan River. If they are taking the overland route to Guizhou or Sichuan, and if they do not want to pass through Yelang, Yongshun or Longshan, then they realize that Zhen Gan is the safest place to unload their goods or luggage and get some rest.

Note: Zhen Gan is modern-day Fenghuang County (Phoenix County).
Yelang is a small ancient kingdom.

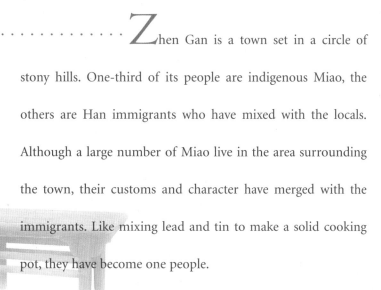

· · · · · · · · · · · · · · · · · Zhen Gan is a town set in a circle of

stony hills. One-third of its people are indigenous Miao, the

others are Han immigrants who have mixed with the locals.

Although a large number of Miao live in the area surrounding

the town, their customs and character have merged with the

immigrants. Like mixing lead and tin to make a solid cooking

pot, they have become one people.

There is the feel of the *Tales of the Arabian Nights* about the place, in the people's hearts, and in the very appearance of the town. All that is lacking is a scribe to record them. And then there is a volume of anthropology in the place, and a bible, and a… how can I describe it? In fact, I could go on forever. Forgive me.

· · · · · · · · · · · · · · · · · The sun is setting. I stand on the highest

point I can find in the town, surrounded by a myriad of moun-

tains, and look across at the ruins of the watchtowers that

stretch from just outside the town to as far as I can see. I imag-

ine I can hear the sound of beating drums and see the glow of

beacon fires sending warnings across the countryside.

· · · · · · · · · · · · · · · · · · Among the people on the riverbank, you

can often make out the pale faces and slender figures of girls

making eyes at passersby. The small tributary that runs around

the northern edge of Zhen Gan does not return to the Chen

River for another 170 li, just before the river flows into Dong

Ting Lake.

Note: A li is a traditional measure of distance, approximately
equivalent to one-third of a mile or half a kilometer.

Every year, when occasion demands it, the town's families visit the Temple of the Heavenly King. There, depending on their wealth and status, they kill pigs, sacrifice goats and dogs, and offer chickens and fish to the gods. They ask the gods to bless and preserve the fertility of their farmland and the health of all domestic animals, to grant long lives to their descendents, to avert illness, or bless a wedding or a funeral.

The houses have two entrances, one facing the street and solid ground, the other facing the river. These are known as stilt houses. Where the houses look out over the river, the householders lean on their windowsills and shout to the passing boatmen.

· · · · · · · · · · · · · · · · · The smoke from cooking fires billows and

subsides, like a white blanket on the hillside. In the distance, the

fields of tiny stumps of harvested rice stalks shine in the sunlight,

as if countless dots have been sprayed onto a piece of paper.

The scenery is like a piece of poetry, spoken with inexpressible

harmony—its beauty is indescribable.

The weather changes with the seasons in a never ending cycle. The shades and colors of the trees, the plants, and even the rocks on the hillsides constantly fluctuate, to compose a different picture for every season. This kaleidoscope leaves me with all sorts of different impressions. Even after sixty or seventy years it gives me the freshest and sweetest pleasure. This is one of the joys of country life I shall never forget.

15

From the riverside houses, in the half-light of dawn, the sharp voices of the womenfolk call out. Their voices sound like the music of a reed pipe, rising above the hubbub. In the cacophony of the river, the sound is both solemn and moving—almost religious.

沈从文和他的湘西

············ The tortuous mountain paths wind into the endless forests, through spectacular rocks and mountain meadows. The shy smiles of the local children peek from under the low eaves of houses snuggled into the sides of the hill. Their guileless grins give the weary traveler a fresh heart.

To describe the warmth and intelligence of a girl from Zhen Gan, I must cast aside all coarse and vulgar language. The girls of Zhen Gan dress themselves in love, beautify themselves with poetry. And that's all there is to it.

沈从文
和他的
湘西

Every house has a loom. Every woman is skilled at weaving cotton and linen. To be part of such an ancient and picturesque citadel, every inhabitant's lifestyle— their very character and spirit—must exist in harmony with the place.

· · · · · · · · · · · · · · · · · The people of Phoenix County are famous for preserving the artistry of the phoenix motif. They design it better and use it far more widely than any other county. Everything with a pattern to it—literally—has a phoenix flying through peony blossoms! The patterns are vigorous, lively, and full of a bold creativity. However, they also have a naiveté to them. The designs are like mountain folk songs handed down from generation to generation. Their birthplace is the very soil.

· · · · · · · According to the season, the locals pay respect to their ancestors and accompany their sacrifices to the gods with many types of sacred songs. At a wedding their songs are congratulatory, consoling at a funeral. The songs are altogether different for manual labor and work in the fields. Whatever the situation, there is a song for it that enchants the ear and delights the heart. And there are count-less courting songs as well!

· · · · · · · · · · · · · · · · · Even if we don't understand any of the original words, or never witness the solemn yet lively scene of a sacrifice to the ancestors, we can still immerse ourselves in the people of Xiangxi and in the deeply spiritual, almost grim, atmosphere of the place. It makes me think that when the great poet Qu Yuan came to Xiangxi almost 2,000 years ago, he must have heard the very same songs.

It is obvious from the way the women of Xiangxi dress that they love beauty. Even if the materials they use are plain—dark homespun cloth, patented, in deep blues and light greens—the cuffs and the trouser bottoms are brightly decorated with beautiful embroidery. Some are original work, some just scraps of printed cloth patched together. An  embroidered apron and a hand-sewn belt add to the effect. The final outfit is an extremely touching expression of simplicity and ruddiness.

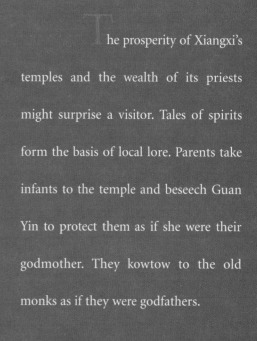

The prosperity of Xiangxi's temples and the wealth of its priests might surprise a visitor. Tales of spirits form the basis of local lore. Parents take infants to the temple and beseech Guan Yin to protect them as if she were their godmother. They kowtow to the old monks as if they were godfathers.

Note: Guan Yin (sometimes Kuan Yin, or Avalokitesvara) is the Buddhist goddess of mercy.

. . . . It is perfectly normal, according to local custom, for a tree or rock to be adopted as a protective spirit for a child. Some of these guardians have as many as fifty charges in their care. Some people pray to cattle pens or to wells to protect their children. Men and gods live in perfect harmony and pass their days together without a hint of discord.

. . . . The eighth day of the second lunar

month is the birthday of the village gods. The streets are filled

with games and festivities. A small space is left for a stage in front

of the temple to the village gods. It is said that the puppet show

is put on for the enjoyment of the old man and wife who are

the village's protective deities. But everyone knows the show is

really for the children.

The day of the village gods' birthday is an excuse for every family to lay out a magnificent spread of food. "Why don't the village gods have a birthday every month?" children ask their mothers, as they greedily eye the white boiled chicken in the middle of the table. Mothers don't give them the benefit of an answer. After the chicken was reduced to bones, ribs, and knuckles, you could still see its grease smeared over our young faces as we watched the puppet show.

· · · · · · · · · · · · · · · · · When the May Festival ends, young and old seem

to gradually forget the weavers' shuttles they have thrown into the river. It is unlikely

anyone would tell you the story behind the shuttles. Only when the spring rains softly

mark the beginning of the May festival in the following year will the drip,

drip of the water remind people of their absent friends and lovers.

The Festival of the Dead falls on the fifteenth day of the seventh lunar month. To Buddhists, the festival is also known as the Ghost Festival. Paper money must be burned for the ancestors and for all dead relatives, close and distant. The girls of every family busy themselves preparing small packets of gold and silver ingots made from tinfoil. At dusk they light them and float them on the river. The mass of tiny, drifting flames lights the way to the western paradise for the spirits of the deceased.

It is New Year. All children love New Year. Some say that many of the more beautiful Chinese festivals were invented just for children. They are not wrong. There may be plenty of festivals that children do not understand, but there is not a single child who does not love New Year the most.

The noodle seller is clacking his bamboo clappers outside our front gate. From deep in his throat comes the soul-stirring cry that never fails to draw customers. From the unique sound of these clappers we can tell that it is old He Er. He sells stuffed dumplings as well. In fact, his dumplings are famous throughout the town. For three coppers you can have both dumplings and noodles. Just remember to dip them in Phoenix brand Xiang Tan soy sauce when you eat them.

Small children love to play. In good weather it was okay for us to go to the hillside. We only had to be careful not to catch cold. We loved to horse around. Never anything serious. People who grow up together, learn together, discover life's pleasures and pain together, become firm friends. Even our fathers didn't object to us hanging out together.

沈从文
和他的
湘西

. . . . Thhe Miao people are very brave and love

a fight. They are innately honest and straightforward. Even

today, the youth of the area have a clearly formed, simple sense

of morality and justice. This morality applies even when they

quarrel or fight. Every evening—except for when it rains—you

will see boys barely twelve years old, bare fisted or

armed with makeshift weapons, tussling and having

a fight.

That the children of Xiangxi are so wild and unrestrained is a deliberate and wise ploy. The taste of success and failure form the basis of a child's education in life. A father can exhaust himself teaching the negative side of life to his son. And for the positive, there are countless spirits and gods. After all, isn't success or failure in the hands of the gods?

· · · · · · · · · · · · · · · · Y ou can either be good at raising fighting

crickets and breeding quails, chickens, ducks, and geese, or bad

at it. What is so unusual is that once someone from Xiangxi gets

their hands on an animal, even ones not usually associated with

fighting, the animals suddenly become fearsome fighting beasts.

There is something amazing about the natural bent for

battle in the children of the place.

That a person's age reflects their attitude to life goes without saying. But the delicate charm and the wild savagery of Xiangxi and its environs will stay with me as I grow old. Watching something as simple as a raft drift down the river seems like an act of god I am dreaming about.

沈从文

和他的

湘西

· · · · · · · · · · · · · · · · · · The day gradually turns to dusk. Wild

Boar Mountain is cloaked with an apron of purple mist just as

the sun fades to a fog. In the sky, red clouds like flower blossoms

chase the sun into the horizon. The sun bids the world farewell.

It is time for the woodcutters to return home, for the

shepherd boys to put the cattle into their pens. A day

is over. For people who live so peacefully, one day

turns into another just as you would turn the page of a book. But

there is no need to ask what you will find on the next page.

My mother was responsible for the early education of my brothers, sisters, and me. That tiny woman was sharp-witted, big-hearted, and wise. I learned much from her. She taught me to read, recited to me the names of Chinese medicinal herbs, taught me how to judge things for myself— a man must make many decisions in life. My bearing and manners were guided by my mother much more than by my father.

My county town was home to 5,000 people. A wooden memorial tablet for the master of the house was enshrined at the gate of every home. I have a vivid memory of how every evening widows and orphans would silently burn incense in front of these shrines and would live on in the absence of the departed. I know the meaning of that silence and how much bitter hardship was contained in it.

It is so peaceful. An everlasting peace in which the townspeople passed their days in pure solitude. A peace to which was added the concerns of daily life and dreams. Living in this small town, every inhabitant had to remember to set aside a portion of their day to ponder mundane matters, their simple loves and hates.

沈从文
和他的
湘西

Sir, do you know what it feels like to play truant from school? If you do not, then you must have gone to a very good school when you were young. But it might also mean that you do not know how to have fun. And if you do not know how to have fun, then, of course, there was no need to play truant.

In the old days, at family-run private schools, we were beaten if we played truant. In fact we would be beaten in any case, even if we did not skip class. But we were only beaten for playing truant if we were found out. There's the catch. If you did not play truant, then there would be at least one occasion every day when the master's cane would crack on your head.

So please reconsider my question, kind sir: Is it better to play truant or not to play truant? Moreover, outside of school there are plays to watch, rivers to swim in, fish to catch, boats to paddle. If you do not mind stiff legs, you can run for miles over the fields. There is dog meat for stewing. Sir, think about all that fun, if you will.

CHAPTER TWO

A SMALL BOOK AND A BIG BOOK

If I were to choose between a good book and this beautiful place, I maintain that I would not read that vacuous fake of a book filled with words. I would read a proper tome whose contents, of real people and events, look—and even smell—good.

My feelings and emotions are constantly flowing. It is as if a fresh, clean wave of water is constantly crashing over me, renewing my impressions of what I see. Of my largely happy young years, the majority of them were spent in close connection with water. You could say my school was a waterside one. My perception of beauty, how I think, both are largely formed by the influence water has had on my life.

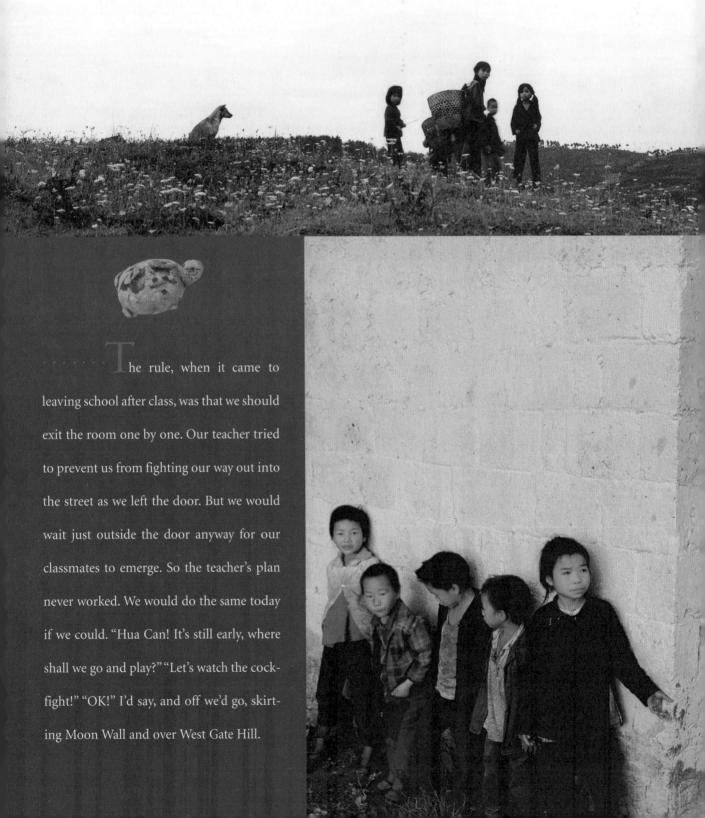

At this private family school I learned how obstinate students could face up to an obstinate teacher by following the example of some older students. We fled from our books and escaped to the outdoors, to be at one with nature. That year formed the basis for my character, my emotional development.

The rule, when it came to leaving school after class, was that we should exit the room one by one. Our teacher tried to prevent us from fighting our way out into the street as we left the door. But we would wait just outside the door anyway for our classmates to emerge. So the teacher's plan never worked. We would do the same today if we could. "Hua Can! It's still early, where shall we go and play?" "Let's watch the cock-fight!" "OK!" I'd say, and off we'd go, skirting Moon Wall and over West Gate Hill.

41

. . . . We used to meet at each other's houses

to play catch the cat. The best place for that game was under-

neath the storehouses in the courtyards. It was very hard to see

into from the outside, yet from inside you could see out perfectly

clearly. If the "cat" was a coward, then he would never dare go

under there so you could be sure nothing could ever happen

to you. Hiding under the storehouse was like escaping into a

foreign concession!

Note: The foreign concessions at the time (before 1949), mostly in coastal cities, enjoyed an
autonomy, which meant they were not governed by Chinese law. Chinese fugitives could
escape punishment *if* they could get into them.

· · · · · · · I learned to climb trees. I learned to fish…. I learned how to skip class. Such physical and temporal pleasures, such useful experiences and delights, are definitely not what the teacher had in mind for us. But they really are all that the school taught me!

We small children in no way neglected to give due reverence to the village gods. We all believed sincerely in their wooden images. We would leave our baskets of school-books in a niche in the base of their temple and when it was time to take them out again, no one would have tampered with them. How many times I entrusted my books to the gods, I have no way of knowing. I did it countless times.

沈从文和他的湘西

· · · · · · · · · · · · · · · · · · The town wall was just outside our gate.

We were always figuring out ways to climb the wall to get a view

out of the town toward the river. On the way to and from school,

we would always go far out of our way, out onto the roads out-

side the town, to see the craftsmen carving new statues of

Buddha and to guess how much gold they had lacquered onto

 them. Or else we would count up how many

new ploughshares the metalworkers had

made, or which family's chickens had hatched new chicks. We

would wander for miles without a worry.

As the days warmed up, the loquats turned yellow and ripened. On the hills there were all kinds of berries, and if you went to Nan Hua Mountain, you could climb trees and stuff yourself with cherries. Thanks to nature's irresistible invitation to enjoy its fruits, I would be forced to kneel for hours, both at home and at school, as a punishment. And still I skipped class!

. . . . We all knew how to climb trees. Part of

the ritual was that you could never be left behind. Even if those

who were at the top of a tree were about to come down, you still

had to climb up to match them. Once you got up there, you

could exhaust your strength hanging upside down, or jump from

as high as possible. But the point was not to show off. Even if you

were entirely alone, there was an innate urge to compete.

It really was as if we were possessed by monkey spirits.

When we went down to the river, we would stash our clothes under a rock on the riverbank, and then a whole day of playing in the water would begin. It was like a festival. Everyone did exactly what they pleased, played whatever game came into their head. There was a weir there, half stopping the water. Altogether the river was split in three at this point. One channel ran along the rocky dam of the weir and into the grain mill, one channel was navigable by boats, and the final one flooded over the weir in a crazy foaming mess.

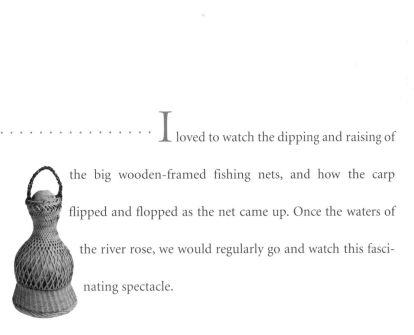

I loved to watch the dipping and raising of the big wooden-framed fishing nets, and how the carp flipped and flopped as the net came up. Once the waters of the river rose, we would regularly go and watch this fascinating spectacle.

I also used to pass by a shop that sold funeral objects and rented out sedan chairs for weddings. There was white-faced Wu Chang, blue-faced Yama, fish and dragons, sedan chairs, the Golden Boy and the Jade Girl. Every day I could work out how many people were getting married, count the funerary objects, see how many times they had been used since they were made, and see if they had changed at all.

Note: Wu Chang is the Grim Reaper, Yama is the King of the Underworld, and the Golden Boy and Jade Girl are attendants of Taoist immortals.

沈从文
和他的
湘西

· · · · · · · · · · · · · · · · · W e only had to sneak a little way off our

route to go and see the paper makers. There we could watch

them using a water-powered grinder to pound to bits rice straw

and tiny chips of bamboo. Then they used a fine bamboo mesh

to ladle out the pulp to make paper.

The things we loved to watch but also that terrified us the most were the grinding stone and the water wheel at the grain mill on the dam above the south stream of the river. The mill was run by Fifth Uncle. That mill stone, fixed on its axis of the wooden beam, just ground and ground and ground, on and on.

沈从文
和他的
湘西

When we played on this bank of the river, we could watch the water wheels on the other side. The big ones cover an area as broad as ten mats used for drying grain. The smaller ones are still at least as big as four mats. If you were not careful when you stood near the water wheels, you'd get a good soaking. The wheels are driven by water, and they make a racket too. The water gets scooped up from the river and then channeled off to irrigate the fields. Watching the wheels working never bored us.

· · · · · · · Yun Yun and Nuo Nuo are digging up sand and making sand castles and mud cannons. Or else they are collecting chips of broken roof tiles to play ducks and drakes with. Who can tell? Splashing in the water is even more fun. "Come on Mangzi! I'm gonna dive! Watch!" No sooner has he bent at the knees than Zhao Xiang has disappeared from view. Ha ha!

Here is an interesting corner of Mao Di's home. Everything is laid out like any other household, as it should be. In this room are the kitchen stove, barrels, small and large vats and jars, and bamboo household containers. Thanks to Mao Di's mother, everything is in perfect order, neat and tidy. It is a typical example of a local household.

沈从文
和他的
湘西

Every day I had to run around the whole town, and cross the famous—in Xiangxi at least—bridge that was approximately one li long. On the other side, facing the river, is Huang Jia Street. All the shopkeepers recognized me. And I knew them all too: the tailor, the silversmith, South Paper Shop, the tobacconist.... Wherever I went, everyone would shout out a hello, and I would stop and chat or mess around with them.

Note: A li is a traditional measure of distance, approximately equivalent to one-third of a mile or half a kilometer.

沈从文
和他的
湘西

. . . . Toward the end of the bridge were grocery stores, rows of butchers' chopping blocks, firework shops, tailors, barbers, cloth merchants, and salt traders. Every time I was taken to see the physician outside the Temple of Well-Being, I had a chance to wonder at those stalls and shops. I loved the end of that bridge. There you could see a complete cross section of society squeezed into one space. And there I learned all about all the various kinds of trade and industry, and the people who practiced them.

When it poured rain all night, right through until morning, all the buckets, pails, and barrels that had been put out under the eaves would be overflowing with rainwater by dawn. Catching that water saved us from calling in Old Jiang, who used to sell water from house to house. The bamboo leaves that wrapped up zhongzi were washed in those barrels of water.

Note: Zhongzi: Glutinous rice and savories wrapped in a bamboo leaf and boiled.

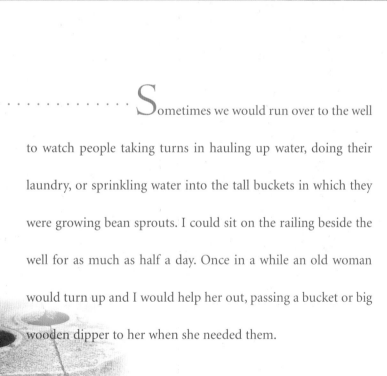

Sometimes we would run over to the well to watch people taking turns in hauling up water, doing their laundry, or sprinkling water into the tall buckets in which they were growing bean sprouts. I could sit on the railing beside the well for as much as half a day. Once in a while an old woman would turn up and I would help her out, passing a bucket or big wooden dipper to her when she needed them.

My heart needed new sounds, new colors, new flavors, or else it would stop beating. I was always looking for new experiences that were outside the normal realm of life. All that I have learned I have consumed and digested from direct experience. I could never have picked that up from a textbook or a clever explanation.

. . . . If you let your spirit soar, unfettered, then

you will come closer to the secrets of nature. I climb a hill.

A river runs along one side of it. Deep in thought I stretch out

on the ground, quite alone. Dreams flood into my head like a

limitless torrent. The real world that immediately

surrounds me seems so solid, so sturdy.

. . . . I must have spent about a year and a half in this residence, which is now the local government office. It was here in the garden that I enjoyed a peaceful and fragrant summer. Upstairs I discovered, in two massive bookcases, a complete set of novels translated by Lin Shu: Dickens's *Oliver Twist*, *Bleak House*, *The Old Curiosity Shop*, *Hard Times*, and more. All of these I read beside the flower-covered trellis on a little platform.

My feelings have always been free flowing, never coalescing into anything solid, like a pure, clear wave of water washing through me. My largely idyllic childhood was pretty much inseparable from water. My "formal" education had a great deal to do with water. How I really learned to think, to appreciate beauty, to understand mankind, was thanks largely to water.

沈从文和他的湘西

. . . . The pale rays of the afternoon sun brush
a mountaintop and stir my emotions, as do the stones beneath
the water of the river. They are round and multi-colored like the
pieces of a Chinese chess set. In my heart there seems to be no
trace of murkiness. A clear light shines through it and out again,
and illuminates all creatures, all the earth. It shines on
the men towing the boats and the small boats themselves.
I love them all so much, with such an intense love. My feelings
have long since bonded themselves inseparably to the scenery
and the sounds of my spiritual home.

Beauty always makes people sad. I might
to all intents and purposes be very happy, but I still use the word
"sadness" for it. In fact, often, when I see such scenery, I will
remain silent for a long time. I wish I had someone with me to
talk to. I wish that person were a good friend, and that
together we could appreciate the scene.

湘西 和他的 沈从文

Along the riverside one can hear the soft sound of human voices, the beating of reed fans, and tobacco pipes being tapped empty on the side of a boat. In the deep of the night, shooting stars leave sparkling trails across the heavens. The sounds from the riverbank rise up and linger like voices from the depth of history. For all my life, I will never forget such night scenes.

· · · · · · · · · · · · · · · · Here again comes the oarsman's song.

It is more like poetry. When I hear such a song, my heart trembles. It seems as if the song is being sung for me, or else for love.

But in fact it is a working song, sung purely for the

pleasure it gives the singer.

The fate of each and every person is pre-ordained. That I know. But there are some things that happened in my past that will always gnaw at my heart. If I speak of them, you will think that I am just telling another story. No one can understand what it means to be oppressed throughout your life by the pressure of so many experiences. Nor can you understand in what state of mind that person must live every day.

沈从文
和他的
湘西

· · · · · · · · · · · · · · · · · The scenery is unutterably secluded and
beautiful, so beautiful it is almost oppressive. That is how I feel
and will always feel. We have no choice: We must go and listen to
those songs that seem to come from a magic flute, just as we
cannot not miss those deeply loved familiar sights and
sounds of the place. We drift farther and farther from
them. Those songs ring like parting laments in the ears
of us youths, as we depart our homes seeking knowledge and the
fulfillment of our dreams in another world.

To see the river flowing all day and night,
eternally, over those rocks and sandbanks, the driftwood floating
on its surface, the flotsam and jetsam of old river vessels, it all
brings to my mind one melancholy word: "history."

沈从文
和他的
湘西

· · · · · · · · · · · · · · · And so one day, I closed the book on

that chapter in my life. I left my pale-faced cousins. I said good-

bye to my prospective fathers-in-law, who always asked me

whenever seeing me, "So how's the poetry going?" I said good-

bye to those four tall and slender girls, their eyes lacquer black

 and hair in braids, and to my poor mother and other

sisters. I bade them all farewell.

沈从文
和他的
湘西

I have lived in a city for fifty or sixty years now, but all that time I have remained a countryman at heart. I have never grown accustomed to city life. I terribly miss the Yuan River and the people who lived alongside it. In spirit I will always be with them both.

Despite the fact that I have long since left those waterways, the majority of the stories that I have written has been based on them. Of all my works, the ones that have given me the most satisfaction are the ones that take as their undercurrent the lives of the boat people and the rivers. The characters that inhabit my stories are all based on the real people I knew who lived beside or worked upon the rivers. If my stories are melancholy, then they are melancholy thanks to the lingering image, formed over fifteen years, of the overcast sky and drizzle-soaked days of the south. And if I say anything interesting or worth remembering in my books, then that is because it was first said by someone who lived beside the rivers of Xiangxi.

CHAPTER THREE

THE LONG RIVER

············· Apart from tales from another time and another people, of men hacking each other to death on whichever battlefield, we will never find in history books the knowledge that we really seek. But these rivers! They can tell us stories of a past score years, and their joys and sorrows! See the small gray fishing boats, crowded on their tops and their rails with silent cormorants that dive lazily into the water? Or on the rocky riverbank, those men pulling boats upstream, their backs slightly bent? These things seem to have absolutely nothing to do with history. But a hundred years ago, or a hundred years from now, nothing has changed, nor will it change. These people lead such honest and simple lives, yet they carry the burden of their own destinies, and those of their children, and thus they live on, through—and transcending—history.

The first person who traveled on these waters, as a passenger on a small boat like this, and who appreciated them and put that into writing, must have been the mad Qu Yuan, of the Chu Dynasty, as he went into exile. He wrote: "I set out from Wangzhu. Tonight I will rest in Chenyang." And if it is worthwhile quoting a few more lines of his poems, how about: "White clover clusters the banks of the Yuan, lilies crowd the Li." When we read, "I embark upon the Yuan," we can only assume that he sat on a boat just like this one, and set off upstream to Yuanzhou, where fragrant flowers luxuriantly blossom.

沈从文

和他的

湘西

. . . . How inexpressibly stunning it all is.

The deep black rocks that line the banks into the distance, the

fragrant flowers that make up banks of color along the river's

edge, the tiny currents and eddies in the water. Had it not been

for such beautiful scenery, Qu Yuan, even if he had gone even

madder, would never have been able to write such

beautiful poetry.

There are some people who, weary of a land-bound existence, go to the forest to cut down a few good trees and saw them into planks. They buy thirty or fifty pounds of nails "as long as an old crow's beak"—as they say in these parts. Then they find themselves a hundred odd pounds of rough hemp, which they plaster with several hundred pounds of tung oil and lime. Thus, using the methods of their forefathers, and following long established designs, they build themselves a sturdy boat on the bank of the river.

沈从文 和他的 湘西

The river that flowed past the town used to flood with spring rains every April or May. On the swollen waters, the varnished boats looked even brighter than normal. The songs of the oarsmen tumbled down on the rushing flood, one after the other. The long rectangular rafts of fallen trees, manned at the corners by ten or so stout fellows, would be heaved downriver by their oars, their strokes eased by the high waters. If you happened to cross the river on a small ferry boat, and chanced to look up, all around you would see mountains, stacked up, row after row, for as far as the eye can see, like a painting.

沈从文
和他的
湘西

· · · · · · · · · · · · · · · · · · Before preparing to weigh anchor or cast off, it was vital to

ensure that man and gods would work and travel in perfect harmony, and that the journey

would be a propitious one. Drums and gongs were beaten, paper money and incense were

burned on the prows of the boats. White cooked pork was offered to the gods and firecrackers

set off. The ceremony and the songs bring to mind the "Songs of the South," and how they came

into being two thousand years ago. The ceremonies and rites that the "Songs" accompanied so

long ago still exist. Thus do history and modernity complement each other.

The boats moored along the bank are packed tightly together. It is impossible to count the masts. Short ones and tall ones reach up for the sky at all angles. The ropes and hawsers seem to have tangled themselves into a giant knot. People stand on the rails and decks of the boats. Their clothes are green and blue and mostly just trousers and simple undershirts. Long-stemmed tobacco pipes poke out from long sleeves. Forearms and ankles are exposed to the cool breeze. The men's calves are covered with a thick downy hair, just as a child imagines the limbs of goblin slaves in a demon's cave.

沈从文 和他的 湘西

Small gray fishing boats, on whose decks and sides crowd black and silent cormorants, paddle lazily downstream. On the rocky riverbank men pull boats upstream, their backs slightly bent. These things seem to have absolutely nothing at all to do with history. But a hundred years ago, or a hundred years from now, nothing has changed, nor will it change. These people lead such honest and simple lives, yet they carry the burden of their own destinies, and those of their children, and thus they live on, through—and transcending—history.

When the wind rises and the rain starts to fall, simple awnings are erected over the decks. People sit under them and listen to the sound of the rain pattering and the wind rustling. The wind hums across the tops of the wavelets in the river. The boats are bound together and depend on each other for support, yet they constantly bump and grind each other. Such is a common sight along the reaches of the Yuan River. To the people who live on the river, this weather is nothing out of the ordinary. They do not relish it. Nor do they resent it. This is their life on the river, and nothing can provoke them into feeling either way about it, love or hate.

. . . . The more time you pass on the wide

river, the broader your view of life becomes. It is common to

bring a wife down to the river to tend your fire, cook for you, and

raise children on your boat. After a couple of years, if your luck

has been kind, and your boat holds together, maybe you'll be

able to save up a few silver dollars and buy a boat with a few cab-

ins and a good pair of oars. That's why some people put

down roots on dry land, while others just keep roving

along the waterways.

· · · · · · · When this kind of rain falls, light though it may be, upriver from Chenzhou it is known as the "half way water." Over the hundred-odd miles above Chenzhou, the raftsmen and loggers take advantage of this natural force to set off down river. When they get as far as the spot facing Wusumu Pass, they all come together again and a happy but hectic frenzy of work begins.

A passing stranger, no matter how hard he tried, could never count the number of boats as they ply down the river. There is an old river warden though, in the fifth district, who can not only count the boats but also keep track of their sequence, as well as remember what each tiny boat and each individual boatman looks like. He holds sway over the entire stretch of river. To those small boats, his supreme power is greater than a Chinese emperor's or president's!

. . . . Let us talk for a while only of the boats moored up against the banks of the river. They are long and narrow and sharp like a knife. They line up along the river, and then the line becomes a chain. They squeeze in together, each prow facing the bank, like a rank of soldiers. Sir, I should warn you that though they might look from a distance like a smart regiment on parade, when you get up close, you will see that they are

 nothing but a shambles of all different ages, uniforms, and weapons! What a motley crew!

Every evening, as the sun sinks through the twilight into the earth, its last rays linger from below the horizon on the evening clouds and warm them into a deep purple glow. A large group of freighters is passing down the river and at dusk pulls in to the riverbank. Through the evening mist that covers the whole river, the sharp sound of the boatmen singing seems to float across the water. The sound at once seems so fine and so noble.

沈从文
和他的
湘西

. . . . The groans, the sighs, the whining. The

exhaustion and the pain that cuts sharper than a knife. How to

take all that and describe it in as few words as possible? Perhaps

it is better, if it means anything, to turn to the line so well known

to men of letters: "To hear the cry of the boatman and the creak

of his oar is far superior to the sound of frogs croaking

on the riverbanks."

As the waters rise, the river warden becomes even busier than usual. It is his responsibility to inspect every inch of the water. Are there any boats where the parents have gone and left their child alone, crying for his milk? Is anyone having an argument that needs breaking up and settling? Is there a risk that an unattended boat might break from its mooring?

沈从文
和他的
湘西

With thirty-seven years' experience of 700 odd li of river, its rising and falling, its changes of course over the years, the warden can clearly name every beach, every pool, every rock—if that rock is big enough to have a name. And he can tell you the stories behind them all, too.

Notes: The holes in the rocks are caused by thousands
of years of boatmen's poles.
A li is a traditional measure of distance, approximately
equivalent to one-third of a mile or half a kilometer.

But he is getting old. His strength will soon desert him. For him, it is now impossible to even consider competing against the younger men or think of traveling as far as he wants along the waterways. He has returned to live out his days on the water because he wants to forget the sorrows of his past life. Like a farmer plucks a bad radish out of the earth, or the leftovers of his amaranth, he wants to throw his bad memories out into the river. He wants to see them washed away with the current.

A cooking fire burns on the stern of every boat. Over it red rice is boiled in a cast-iron pot. Once the rice is done, oil is heated up in a wok, and with a fierce sizzling the vegetables are thrown in to be stir-fried. Once everything is ready, everyone squats down on the deck. After three or four or even five bowls, their bellies are full and it will already be dark and time for sleep.

· · · · · · · · · · · · · · · · · Once again I hear the hauntingly beau-

tiful sound of a song. This time it is sung by small children. It is

delicate and enchanting. If you should ever hear such a song,

you will remember it for as long as you live. It is like

poetry. Such music penetrates the ear, and your heart,

like no other.

If you are a landscape artist, then you should compose your scene like this. First, get into your head the very essence of the famous line: "At the lonely ferry crossing, the boat lies still." Now paint a white pebble beach on the left—the west side—of your picture. Then you are getting close to a true representation. I know not for how long, but paintings of the river have always been thus. And in that scene, there I am too. Without a care in the world, idle from dawn till dusk, surrounded by the myriad mountains. Warmed all day by the sun, I have fallen asleep!

湘西 和他的 沈从文

A visitor cannot help but let out a soft sigh as he tries to describe the scene—the haze of mist and the lightly falling rain. The local weather often seems to envelop the mountains, the water, and the people in this amorphous grayness that is neither rain nor mist. And with such weather comes an irrepressible yet slight sense of desolation and misery. Yet, you can feel the omnipresence of the brilliance of life.

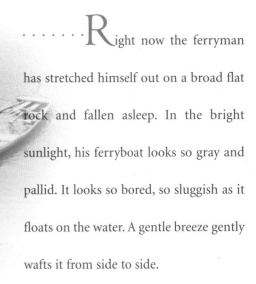

Right now the ferryman has stretched himself out on a broad flat rock and fallen asleep. In the bright sunlight, his ferryboat looks so gray and pallid. It looks so bored, so sluggish as it floats on the water. A gentle breeze gently wafts it from side to side.

"Guan Yin is not afraid of traveling a bit to satisfy her heart's desire! Why, every day she goes all the way from the Purple Bamboo Forest to the South Ocean, just to wash her feet! Now how far is that I ask you!" The ferryman pushes the boat off with a languid shove as he turns to chat with the passengers. "I am telling you it's true. And I also know it's true that the Emperor Xuan Tong has abdicated. Yuan Shi Kai has evil designs on taking over power but our own Cai E from Hunan, he ain't convinced Yuan is the right man. You know what, he went and kicked over the throne when Yuan was about to sit on it and gave him a piece of his mind! You get to know things when you get old like me, I'm telling you. There ain't much I haven't heard." And the passengers laugh at his ranting.

Note: Cai E was the provincial governor of Yunnan, but a native of Hunan, the province that includes Xiangxi. He refused to recognize Yuan Shi Kai when Yuan declared himself emperor (having been president of the Republic of China). In 1915 Cai E retired to Yunnan, where he raised an army that eventually defeated Yuan's forces.

· · · · · · · · · · · · · · · · · The boats sway back and forth on the

crystal-clear wavelets. They seem to have minds of their own and

would, if they were not tied up, take themselves off to play on the

water like children. Again I look over to the far side of the river,

at the flat ridge that runs along it, washed by the moonlight into

a pale grayness. A layer of white mist, like a layer of milk, covers

the lower reaches of the river. I can see a speck or two

of light occasionally shining through it.

It is incredibly silent when the boat heaves

to, as if all sound has been frozen into nothingness, just like

when the air freezes before snow starts to fall. All you can hear is

the water slapping against the hull as the current ever so softly

drags it downstream. In fact, you do not hear the noise.

You feel it.

沈从文
和他的
湘西

· · · · · · · · · · · · · · · · Τhat is how beautiful life is along the two

sides of this river. I can only sketch for you a rough outline. I will

probably never have the skill to add the colors, the sounds, the

light. In fact, you should come to the river and see for yourself.

If you do see it, then in one instant you will witness more than I

could ever describe for you. I tell you, you could not even dream

of a place like this. When you climb aboard a boat yourself,

you will be bedazzled by the beauty of the river.

I find it hard to bear, now that I realize how nature has cursed me with such ignorance. The spoken and written word are simply too impoverished. But if you could be there, and see and hear, among the human cacophony and the cocks crowing, the men hammering on their upturned boats, bashing lime into the cracks in the hulls, you would realize that no words could ever describe such an idyllic scene.

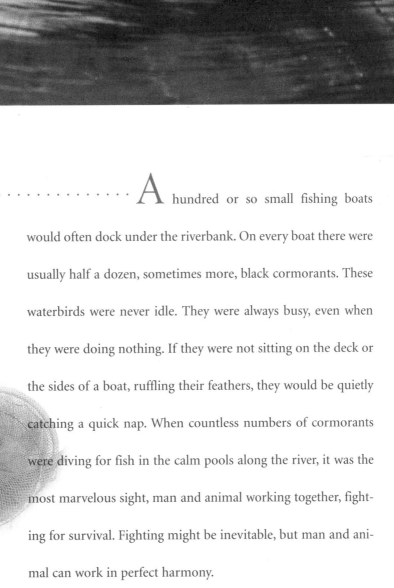

. . . . A hundred or so small fishing boats would often dock under the riverbank. On every boat there were usually half a dozen, sometimes more, black cormorants. These waterbirds were never idle. They were always busy, even when they were doing nothing. If they were not sitting on the deck or the sides of a boat, ruffling their feathers, they would be quietly catching a quick nap. When countless numbers of cormorants were diving for fish in the calm pools along the river, it was the most marvelous sight, man and animal working together, fighting for survival. Fighting might be inevitable, but man and animal can work in perfect harmony.

One of the more straightforward customs of such a border region was prostitution. And it really was very simple and unsophisticated. New customers would have to pay in advance, and only then would the door be shut and the real business be started inside. Regulars could pay when they liked, and sometimes not at all. For the most part the girls relied on traders from Sichuan for their livelihood. But in their hearts they were fonder of the river workers.

For the girls who worked from boats, just like anywhere else in the world, they considered themselves engaged in a "trade." It was for "business" that they came to this place. As for their status, they were just like any other tradesman, just so long as they behaved ethically and looked after their health. These girls often came down from the country, from farming homesteads. They left their villages, their millstones, and their cows. They left behind young and fit husbands. They were enticed away by a friend or new acquaintance and ended up on a boat, in the "trade."

I felt that their dreams and their misery were almost sacred. I never used money or other means to insinuate myself into their fate, or to interfere with the cycle of joy and pain of their lives. As I disembarked from one of their boats once, and was walking along the riverbank, I heard someone singing the song "My Fantasy Lover." Although the tune was so base and vulgar, the singer's voice was clear and sharp. I knew out of whose mouth the song was coming and for whom it was sung. I stood dumbly in the cold winter wind for a long time, listening.

It was the custom. When a girl left her life in the village, her husband was quite aware that she was going into a business for profit, and what kind of business it was. He understood that she was still his wife, that the sons she bore belonged to him, and if she made any money, there would be some for him, too.

It is the time of day when all lights and noises fade away except for the red lights on the water and the sound of the fishermen. Those lights and sounds denote the deadly battle between the fishermen and the fish in the water. It has been fought on these waters for many thousands of years and thus will it continue every night for many thousands more to come.

湘西 和他的 沈从文

· · · · · · · · · · · · · · · · · The sound of the fishermen's clappers is
unique. In such an otherwise peaceful setting, if a young girl
should hear it she would, for sure, be both delighted and frightened. You could say the sound is like a beautiful poem. Yet it is
also like a mystery-laden Taoist incantation that
grips you like a spell and leaves you dumbstruck.

The moon is growing even brighter in the night sky. In its light, small boats cluster up close to the bigger ones, and cries rise up from those boats where traders are selling pork knuckles and noodles. The way they shout out their wares it seems as if they are singing just for the joy of it, not because they are trying to sell anything. The slapping of their paddles on the water sounds like music written especially to accompany the song.

沈从文 和他的 湘西

Sixteen years ago, this quay on the river-
side taught me much. It let me understand about the ways of
men, and it gave me my dreams. If today I were to return and
review all the lessons that it taught me, I fear that the dream-
land of youth that it once inhabited will have vanished.

I climb out of the back of the awning on the boat to sit in the sun. I look at the river and imagine its current washing away, wiping clean, the accounts that I have outstanding with this place, with this river. I have been away from this place for sixteen years now. Those sixteen years have passed in a flash. I think of all the changes that have happened in those sixteen years and let out a heartfelt sigh. Again and again I let out that sigh. This place is my second home.

沈从文和他的湘西

· · · · · · · · · · · · · · · · · · The history of Chinese literature would

not be the same if, two thousand years ago, Qu Yuan had not

been exiled from the state of Chu, and, in his fit of madness,

come wandering to this bizarre yet beautiful corner of China, to

witness and experience its soul-stirring landscape. Nor would

Chinese literature be what it is today if later scholars and

writers never had the good fortune to be able to read the

Nine Songs of Qu Yuan, inspired by that trip.

沈从文
和他的
湘西

My works are slightly different from those of other writers of my generation. From the very earliest of my pieces, I have drawn predominantly on my birthplace as a source of inspiration; the long and winding Yuan River, where I was born and bred. It is from the Yuan River, her tributaries, dozens of townships and hundreds of jetties that I learned of humanity's joy and pain. The vistas of the place left a lasting impression on me. So I thought I would try to bring all that together in a collection of prose poems.

There are people in this world who dream of building cathedrals or towering pavilions, on foundations of sand or water. I am not one of those. I would simply like to build a small Greek-style temple. I would choose a mountain as the foundation and would build it by piling up good solid rocks. It would be sturdy yet exquisitely designed, well proportioned. Although it would be small, it would not be dainty or "cute" as such. This kind of architecture is my ideal. And I would dedicate this temple to Humanity.

CHAPTER FOUR

BORDER TOWN

Sir, if you allow yourself to be absorbed by this humble work of mine, maybe you will gain something from it. No matter what it is, be it a mild concern, a little happiness, a touch of melancholy, or even an unbearable feeling of bitterness, rest assured it will only be a small dose of that sensation. Even if you have no preconception whatsoever, you must still, bit by bit, come to feel the mood of the people about whom I write, and eventually to also empathize with me, the author. I do hope this will not make you feel as if you have sunk to our level!

I know these people's happiness and pain. I share in them in fact. It makes me cry and yet it makes me smile too, to witness them live out their days in such a way. Even though I am so far away from them, at the same time I feel so close to them. It is just like reading a story about the lives of Siberian peasants. It makes you feel, as you close the book, an unspeakable woe. Today I rely not only on my imagination to comprehend how these people live and how they act, but I have also turned to my own experience, to my own past, to find their true spirit.

My writings have dealt with a wide range of social topics. But the affairs of the villages and small towns along the tributaries and valley of the Yuan River are something I am very familiar with. The loves and hates, joys and suffering, lives and emotions of the people of the river valley all possess their own outstanding traits. My own fate is inextricably linked with this place. I am inseparable from it.

沈从文
和他的
湘西

T his is the distant exile to which the ancient

Southern Tribes of Jing were driven by the Han invaders. The Jing originally came

from Yunmeng, in the marshes surrounding Dongting Lake. There were five small

rivers there and thus the people became known as the "Five River Tribe." According

to the annals, the Han general Ma Yuan came here to conquer the tribe but he was

surrounded, besieged and died at Hutou Mountain, which lies in the heart of the

Yuan River basin. And that is why every provincial town in the maze

of valleys around the Yuan has a Fubo memorial hall.

Note: Fubo is an honorific bestowed on Ma Yuan by Zhugeliang, his commander-in-chief.
It literally means "Calmer of the Stormy Seas," and it was later often conferred on successful military leaders.

115

Cha Dong sits with its back to the mountain and faces the river. Where it backs onto the mountain the town wall climbs and winds along the slope like a long snake. On its riverside there is a stretch of quay where a motley collection of covered boats is anchored. Boats going downstream take cargoes of tung oil, black salt and galls for dye. Boats arriving upstream deliver loads of both finished and unspun cotton, bolts of cloth, and seafood.

湘西 和他的 沈从文

. . . . Usually, when I think about Luxi county,

the songs the boatmen sing as they pull on their oars together

come to my mind. The memory soaks into my heart like fine

rain, pervading it. This county has a special place in the story

of my life. When I think of it I feel both bitterness and

happiness.

If there is a quay beside the river, then for sure there will be crowds of parasites living off others: officials holding sinecures, widows who get by on the interest they make from small loans, prostitutes who are blessed with big breasts and buttocks. There'll be a teahouse where you can play ma jiang or Chinese chess. There is never a shortage of spare time or idlers ready to waste it in social intercourse. The small quays along the river are bursting with the vitality of this sort of low life.

· · · · · · · · · · · · · · · · This jetty is called X Village and comes

under the administration of Y Prefecture. It sits in the center of

the You River valley network. Two hundred li downstream you

come to the large river port of Yuan Ling, where the You and

Yuan rivers meet. Go upstream two hundred li and you get to

Cha Tong, on the border of Sichuan and Hunan, and just down

the road from You Yang. If you are well read you will

know what I mean if I call the place, "The two cultural

centers of the You."

Note: A li is a traditional measure of distance, approximately
equivalent to one-third of a mile or half a kilometer.

Looking south from the north bank of the river, at the mountains, the bamboo groves, the copses, the temples, pagodas, houses—it all seems so perfectly laid out. The higher mountains in the distance look like a man-made screen. They glow with indigo blues and emerald greens when they are not hidden from view by the misty rain and shifting clouds. In the mysterious half-light of dawn or dusk, as you look at them, you can easily imagine gods and spirits cavorting on dragons and racing across rainbows.

. . . . As the waters of the river rise with the

season, so do the opium boats and floating brothels moor them-

selves closer to the shore. They line themselves up beneath the

stilts of the riverside houses. In the Four Seas Spring Teahouse,

the drinkers lean up against the window frames and look out

onto the river. They can either gaze across the river at the

picturesque "light rain and red peach" scene of the pagoda on

the opposite bank, or they can watch the girls down

below lighting opium pipes for their customers.

The riverside teahouses are stacked so tightly on the bank that it is easy to shout up at a friend in an upper story window or down to one on the street. People exchange friendly greetings or else swear, brag, and joke with each other. Once you have paid the bill for your tea, you leave by the wet and stinking dirty passageway and board your boat.

Come to the end of the streets, just outside the downtown area and you will find the lower reaches of a long pond called Silk Thread Pond. The story has been passed down from generation to generation that the pond is so deep that if you took the thread from a jin of silk, it would only just reach the bottom. Towering above the two sides of the long pond, like a screen, are precipitous cliffs of many different hues. Day and night, there must be at least a hundred fishing boats floating on the long stretch of water, all crowded with cormorants. As the boats pull themselves along the water, the beauty of the scene relieves the picture of hardship contained in it.

Note: A jin is equivalent to approximately one pound.

Two mountains are emerald green with bamboo. I am struck dumb by the beauty of the stilted houses on the high banks. The way the scenery rises into the distance, wrapped in smoke and clouds, inspires me deeply! Normally, I can easily envisage a beautiful scene and commit it to paper, but the beauty of this one defeats me. A thousand writers of the Song and Yuan dynasties, and all their peach blossom springs, could never compare to this sight.

Note: A peach blossom spring refers to a mythical paradise that can only be stumbled on and never found again.

The source of the Dong River is high up in Miao County. All year round, where the Dong joins the mainstream, you can find fifty or sixty of the small and black Dong River boats moored. The boatmen are typical Miao, short and sturdy, full of energy, and each wearing the traditional Miao patterned head cloth and apron around their waist. Some are pale faced and carry themselves quite elegantly. They speak with eloquence and refinement, and have a reputation as fine singers.

沈从文 和他的 湘西

. . . . Night overtakes the whole river. In the

darkness you can see the light of the fires built by the raftsmen

on their rafts, and the lantern light shining from the windows of

the stilt houses. As people wind their way through the rocks on

the riverbank, up to the houses or down to their boats, you can

make out the flickering lights of their torches. At this time of

year, the houses and boats are full of the chatter of voices. And

out of the faint light that shines in the windows of the stilt

houses, you can hear the sound of the girls singing softly. At the

end of each song, the listeners applaud with laughter.

When the mood takes them, the boat-men go ashore to build a fire to sit around and chat. Instead of raising a lantern on the mast they'll use an old piece of rope for a torch and, following its flickering light, leap from the bow onto the shore. Then they'll follow a path through the rocks and climb up the hillside to a familiar spot beside the stilt houses. There they'll encounter old friends and acquaintances and invite them to join them. Any stranger who happens to pass along one of these rivers, or stop beside one of the villages, ceases to be a stranger the minute he sits down beside the fire, on an old wooden plank, and shares it with the locals.

沈从文
和他的
湘西

. . . . The morning sun rises. Gently it corrals the morning ground mist, coerces it and congeals it into a damp cloud that lingers in the town center, and then it disappears altogether. The town's higher rooftops slowly emerge from the fog into the morning sunlight. A pearl-like luster lingers on them like a diaphanous shawl, refracted into many wondrous colors. The scene resembles a haunted palace in a dream. Slowly the mist slips from the eaves to the ground and then vanishes, as if by magic.

. . . . In the scattered settlement next to Da Ao

Village there are more than two hundred homes. Presiding over

them all, in the most senior position, is the Heavenly Buddha,

after whom is the God of Rain. Next in the hierarchy comes

the village headman and the guardian gods of the village

itself. Finally, there is the warden in charge of the village

threshing ground.

There is a place down by the river that is really quite beautiful. Its name is Oil Creek. The old wall that once encompassed it is still standing. There must have been an oil mill here once. It seems crazy that someone once made oil here, in a place that is so suffused with poetry.

沈从文和他的湘西

. . . . The oil press stands in a corner of the room. The line of thick, coarse wooden pillars and the metal sheets and metal nails all give off a black and oily reflection from the faint light that filters in from the roof, and from the glow of the fire. The scene strikes awe into your heart, as if it was not an oil press but a human press, that terrifying tool of torture from ancient stories.

The smoke from the kitchen fires collects on the rooftops. It dithers and dallies and dips and rises. It comes together finally, in a solid sheet. As dusk approaches it merges with the evening mist to become a curtain that falls on the village at the day's end.

湘西 和他的 沈从文

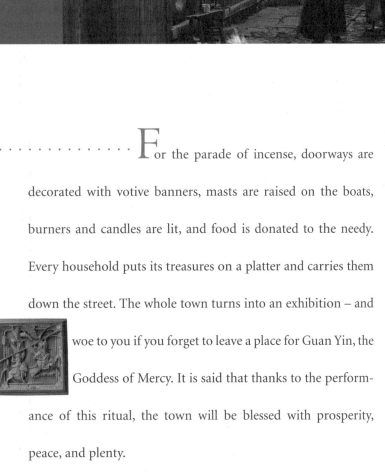

. . . . For the parade of incense, doorways are decorated with votive banners, masts are raised on the boats, burners and candles are lit, and food is donated to the needy. Every household puts its treasures on a platter and carries them down the street. The whole town turns into an exhibition – and woe to you if you forget to leave a place for Guan Yin, the Goddess of Mercy. It is said that thanks to the performance of this ritual, the town will be blessed with prosperity, peace, and plenty.

There are ten or so large willow trees overlooking the water. The long narrow leaves fall on the stream and form a yellow blanket. In the sunlight they look like a shoal of tiny sparkling silver fishes. And under the willows there are a dozen young girls, their heads wrapped in black head cloths, heavy silver earings hanging from their ears. They are washing clothes or vegetables and chatting. It is a blissful scene.

Every available space along the riverbank is covered with white sheets or green vegetables drying in the sun. Every day countless village women will come to the river with bamboo baskets of clothes on their backs. With their beating rods they will beat the clothes clean in the fast flowing water. The thwack and thump of their work echoes off the base of the town's northern wall. When the weather gets hotter, every afternoon at about four o'clock, the river will be packed with naked bodies.

Slowly it turns, and deeply it sings, like

the chief mourner leading the procession at the funeral of time

itself. Anywhere in the world, any place at all, time is forever

being wasted. We should install waterwheels like this every-

where. And then we should add for good measure the sighs and

cries of a tormented and hopeless crowd of men and beasts.

Then see how every new day gobbles up the past one in a mean-

ingless, inescapable cycle.

Everyone who lives in this small town divides their days, one from the other and each within itself. And as they watch time pass, they wait for the joys and sorrows of life to come. But what, if anything, do they really think about life? No one knows.

沈从文 和他的 湘西

· · · · · · · · · · · · · · · · · · · He is remembering his wild days with

his army unit, thinking of the many beautiful girls he has

known, with pale faces and long arched eyebrows. As the under-

currents of fond memories stir his enfeebled old heart, a watery

light leaks into his eyes and burns there with

youthful fire.

· If you heard that he was respected by the townsfolk because

of his duty sounding the watches of the night, then you are being misled. He loves to drop in to

the grain liquor shop tucked inside the archway of the town gate and have a drink. On his way

back he'll generally stagger and stumble and then fall fast asleep in the gutter. When he wakes

up, he grabs his wooden clapper which doubles for a pillow and, like a monk beating a wooden

fish, he clacks and claps his way along the streets. So why do people put up with him? Quite

simply because he is such a friendly old fellow.

$\cdots\cdots\cdots$Immediately after they have come ashore, the musicians start blowing on their suonas. The "wu wu la la" reverberates around the hill. Grandpa and Cui Cui stay on the boat. But their hearts have followed the music ashore, and as far as the music goes, their hearts go too, before the sound dies and they return to the boat.

Note: A suona is a horn—a woodwind instrument.

The old woman soaks up the sun, sitting at the base of the mud wall on a pile made up of the detritus of old beehives that have fallen from the eaves. From the far corner of the house you can hear the sound of someone slowly but surely husking rice with a pestle and mortar. The perfect mise-en-scene makes a touching picture.

He is a good man. He is not pompous or pretentious like the Taoist priests in the town. He is extremely diligent as he sings his sacred songs, performs the holy dances, and prostrates himself. He is neither greedy for money nor does he bully his apprentices. But when it comes to really getting rid of evil spirits or curses, who knows if his Taoist magic actually works or whether he is just conning you out of your money.

When autumn arrives the countryside and the peasants come into their own. Wherever you look, under the eaves of the houses, at the faces of the farmers, across the fields, over the water, everywhere you can see nature completing its cycle. A year is about to come to an end. The world is gearing up for the harvest and preparing to wind down for its winter rest. As winter approaches, the puddles on the muddy roads turn to ice and the first frost turns the country into a dazzling whiteness. The countryside is suffused with the graceful yet severe beauty of winter.

The days of threshing rice are filled with bustling activity. The farmers are happy at the prospect of a bumper harvest. On the one hand they delight in the work of bringing the year to a close, and on the other they are looking forward to a well-deserved rest. The whole village is smiling.

· · · · · · ·Some people have already put their rice into the storehouse. Some have already dehusked the freshly harvested grain and go from house to house offering their neighbors a taste.

145

Among the women of the area, not a few practice the oldest profession known to man. And those who don't are often involved with the boatmen who travel up and down the river, though their liaison is a less commercial one. At this time of year there is much talk and debate as accounts, of both the financial and the purely emotional kind, are settled. Tears mix with laughter, singing and smiles. Some bottle up their resentments, some, through their tears and sniffling, beg for pledges of fidelity in the year to come.

沈从文
和他的
湘西

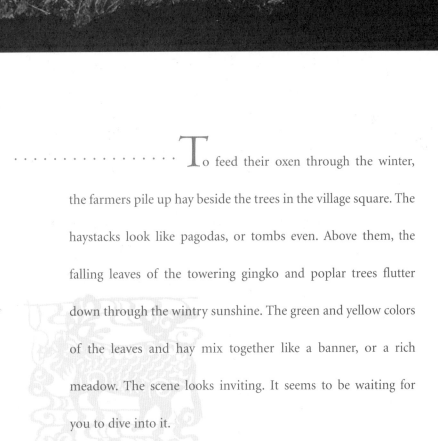

. . . . T̶o feed their oxen through the winter,

the farmers pile up hay beside the trees in the village square. The

haystacks look like pagodas, or tombs even. Above them, the

falling leaves of the towering gingko and poplar trees flutter

down through the wintry sunshine. The green and yellow colors

of the leaves and hay mix together like a banner, or a rich

meadow. The scene looks inviting. It seems to be waiting for

you to dive into it.

· · · · · · · · · · · · · · · · · · · On the day that the theater performance

comes to town, the village folk and people from all around put

on freshly starched clothes, stuff some small change into their

shoulder bags or money belts, and hurry over to the Fu Bo

memorial hall beside Luobo Stream to watch the show. While

the performance is going on, they keep one eye on the action and

wander through the crowd buying snacks and small treats.

沈从文
和他的
湘西

Just slightly off to the left from the center of the room, there is a three hob stove. Where it sits up against the wall, there is a large brick chimney. Beside the stove are a couple of big water vats, three empty water buckets, a cupboard for bowls and a kitchen cupboard made from bamboo hanging on the wall. Over the years the smoke from the stove has stained the wall around it blacker than pitch. Further along that same wall hang all sorts of utensils, shovels, wooden clubs for beating laundry and pitchforks.

Before you hear the drums and gongs of the village fair, there is another racket that you will hear first. "Na Na, where is your mother?" "Hey Granny! Why haven't you brought your grandson along?" "Dai Gou! Quick! Get over here! They're selling salted sunflower seeds!" "Oi, Sister! There's space on a bench right here!"

This is like reading a story about the lives of peasants in Siberia. It makes you feel, as you close the book, an unspeakable woe. Today I rely not only on my imagination to comprehend how these people live and how they act, but I have also turned to my own experience, to my own past, to find their true spirit.

There are massive wooden hooks, bound up with kudzu vines, hanging down from the ceiling beams. They have been used for so long that the grain has been polished out of the wood. And they are so black with use that you can no longer tell which was once tea wood and which teak. (These hooks were specially designed for winter when they were hung with cured meat, dried wild boar meat, and goat meat. Nowadays they are used for hanging baskets of drying chili peppers.)

The days of the summer months pass peacefully and safely. It seems as if the long days of sunshine drive away any ailment that might afflict the locals. The weather is very hot. Everyone sweats. They dilute rice wine with cold water and gulp it down. The days are carefree and the people forget their worries.

It has only been a few times that snow has fallen and the mist risen, that Qingming and Guyu have come and gone. Yet everyone is already saying that Xiao Xiao is a grown-up. It is thanks to the blessing of heaven, the pure cold water, and eating rough grain rice that she has never fallen ill, and developed so fast. Granny might have a temper as sharp as a knife, but the opportunity to cut Xiao Xiao down to size with it has long since passed. The country climate and fresh air, if they cannot alleviate entirely the hardship of life here, at least ensure that people grow up strong and healthy.

Note: Under the traditional Chinese calendar, there are twenty-four seasonal points by which the solar year is divided. Qingming (Pure Brightness) and Guyu (Grain Rain) are two of them. The former usually falls on April 5 or 6 and the latter on April 20 or 21.

沈从文 和他的 湘西

The local old ladies are apt to take pleasure in criticizing anyone who is slender and good-looking: "She is so beautiful that she might have a short life." Nonetheless, no matter how many times they say such a thing to a girl, the fact is they would all be more than happy to have your younger sister (who is slender and good-looking) as their daughter-in-law once they see her.

. . . . It seemed almost magical. As if in the blink of an eye, this orphan has suddenly gone from being a young girl to a grown-up thirteen-year-old. Because they live on the hill among the almost oppressively emerald green bamboo, the old boatman whose family adopted the pitiful young swallow of a girl chose the name Cui Cui for her.

Note: Cui means emerald green.

Third daughter is very small but has long legs. Her mouth is tiny but her teeth are shiny white. Her nose is perfectly formed and her eyebrows are fine, yet with a strong hint of wildness about them. She is black from head to toe, and her character seems to be a little on the dark side too, like a little "Black Princess." As the youngest of all the children, she was given the name Yao Yao.

Note: Yao literally means youngest.

When Qin Feng had her fortune told according to the day of her birth, we all thought it was strange. She would either be a "lady" or a "prisoner." Not only would she jinx her mother, but her later life would be "eventful" too. When Qin Feng heard this, she just pursed her lips and smiled.

When winter arrived, once again they restored the old tumbled down pagoda. But that young man who used to sing under the moonlight will never come back to Cha Dong. His songs used to conjure up the image of spirits and ghosts in Cui Cui's dreams. That is to say, he might never ever come back, or he might be back tomorrow!

沈从文
和他的
湘西

There is a long street alongside the river where you can see countless boatmen and their women. At the end of the street flutter the long streamers of the tax office, on which, in black ink on red cloth, in heavy and formal official characters, are written the words "Tax Office." Hundreds of boats are moored underneath while the owners go ashore to register their cargo. At the other end of the street, the big wall around the oil mill is like a city wall. Oil is milled all year round. The oil makers raise their mallets high in the air and as they swoosh them down, they hum a song.

I have seen so many riverside streets like that. I have learned much from them. I have picked up almost everything I have written in my stories of the river from places like this. I love these places and their people. Their life is so pure that it moves me to tears. I feel so at one with them. I think I must be the first Chinese person to have felt such a compelling interest in them. Yet I am still apart from them. I can never really share their lives. It is

CHAPTER FIVE

SMALL-TOWN STREETS AND MARKETS

strange. I love them so much. And ever since the May the Fourth Movement, I am apparently the only person who seems to have paid any attention to them.

· · · · · · · · · · · · · · · · · · Thereis more than a man can ever tell about this place. If I could make a selection from some of my own writings and use them to try to explain, to describe Xiangxi to the reader, then I could do no better than turn to my work, *Small Town*, something I wrote in a bygone era. But that was a work of fiction, not fact. It is impossible to describe all the details and observations that make up a true and accurate description of Xiangxi. It is like a rainbow, colorful and splendid to everyone who sees it. It is soft, warm, and beautiful. It is close and yet far away. Gather a thousand poets to write a poem about the same rainbow, and there will still be something about that rainbow that is missing from all thousand poems!

Running along the side of every quay by the water is a riverside street. The houses are built half on land and half over the water. Thanks to the limited space, there is no alternative but to use stilts to hold up the buildings.

· · · · · · · · · · · · · · · · · But because there are such houses along

the edge of the river, the boatmen who struggle with the river all

year long, the sick and feeble who cross by the public ferry, and

all other travelers passing through have somewhere to make a

landfall. The houses along the river are a haven where

those exhausted and weary people can find solace.

I feel as if I know so well the houses in the middle of town whose roofs and rafters are all interconnected. And I know the people who live in them too. Even though seventeen years have passed, I still recognize every downtown street and can differentiate the smells of each district.

沈从文 和他的 湘西

T hose riverside streets were my favorite place as a child. All those small stalls and shops were full of surprises. They sold hawsers for boats, toys carved out of hardwood, small fish baskets, little knives, steels for lighter flints, cigarette  holders…the ground was covered with fascinating objects. When I squatted down beside those treasures it was as hard to get me away as it would be to drag a distinguished gentleman away from studying a precious antique.

The general stores mainly sold equipment for boats, as well as various other sundry items. You could say that they were there purely for the benefit of the boatmen. For example, they stocked oil and salt, cloth, leather, and tobacco. But you could also say that without the stores, there would have been no boatmen. It is the same with the teahouses and liquor shops, as well as those houses that supplied a more straightforward "service." If it were not for the boatmen, they would not exist, and vice versa.

沈从文 和他的 湘西

· · · · · · · · · · · · · · · · · This riverside street, being so long, was

full of variety and life. Thanks to the townsfolk carrying pails of

water along it all day and every day, it was always soaked wet and

slippery with the spillage. I would pass along it once or twice a

day at least, and every time I did I would squat down at the

slightest sign of something interesting, be it brand new

or something that had been there for years. I would

hardly notice the daylight fading and before I knew it

dusk would have fallen.

The doors of those whose lives were tied to the river and who lived off the waterfront, were always wide open. You often saw captains of boats, wearing short satin jackets, accompanied by their coarse and uncouth boat hands, entering them. The places looked like teahouses but did not serve tea. Nor were they opium dens, but you could have a pipe in there.

沈从文
和他的
湘西

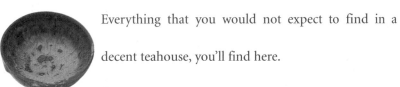

The decoration and state of this teahouse perfectly matches the kind of people who come here. The tables are grimy and greasy with oil. The legs of the wooden benches are too thin and rickety. The cheap blue and white porcelain cups and their lids contain the coarsest of green tea leaves. Everything that you would not expect to find in a decent teahouse, you'll find here.

On market days, business at the herbal medicine shop boomed. When I stood outside the place, I would see lots of people inspecting the medicines. When the owner saw us, he would ask us if we had come to buy a poultice. He was giving away a brand new type. In his opinion a poultice should be stuck on every soldier's leg. He had no idea what kind of people actually needed those silly square things.

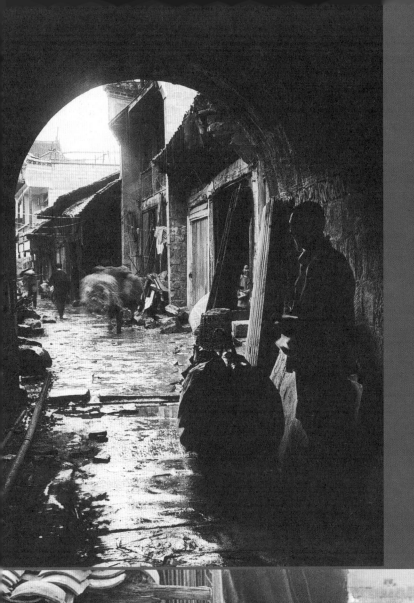

If you sold cakes on this street, then you smacked bamboo clappers together. If you sold sweets, then you hit a copper gong. When these salesmen tried to pull in their customers, they all knew the oldest trick in the book, which was to step into the street and sing out a song with a crazy tune, whose words generally included a reference to the female anatomy. The trick was to make people laugh and get their attention.

I used to love wandering the streets, slowly, like a tourist visiting an historic site, such as the ruins of ancient Rome. Like a tourist, I would study in detail the sights before me. It always seemed to me that I recognized all the faces I saw, and all the sounds that I heard seemed extremely familiar.

Before the dried bean curd maker had even heard the sound of the bugle, he had stopped what he was doing and had gone to see what these latest soldiers looked like. He kept a dog in his bean curd shop, which jumped at the sound of the soldiers' stamping feet and cowered behind his master's legs, where it peeped out at the marching men.

The soldiers were hanging around outside the house's half open door. Through the latticework, their prying eyes sought out the pale faces of the girls hiding inside. In a loud whisper they exchanged opinions on what they had found and made dirty jokes. "Whoa! ... Hey man! Check this one out!" "No no, look over here, there's another!" "Here's one with ponytails!" "I'm in love! I'm gonna marry her!"

You could say that our days passed in blissful happiness. Apart from hanging around at the bean curd shop, drinking bean curd paste and admiring the owner's beautiful daughter, we also often used to go to the main square and watch public executions.

沈从文 和他的 湘西

. . . . People who lived in the stilt houses all had

friends and relatives living and working far away whose return

they keenly anticipated. Every time they heard the sound of a

drum beat, they thought of someone dear to them. For this

festival, of course the majority of the boatmen hurried home.

But many would not make it in time and would gather together

and pass the celebration somewhere halfway there. For them

the party would be half happy and half sad, and their families

would likewise stop and quietly think of them in pauses in the

merriment.

Many families kept dogs. The animals walked along the street, ahead or behind their owner, wagging their tails. Every so often they would stop and raise their leg against the wall of a house and mark their territory with a stream of urine. Then they rushed to catch up with their owner. The streets were never empty. There was always someone there, or something going on.

As evening approaches, the women who spend every day walking the town's streets and walls, barefoot, with their baskets of produce head for home, one after the other. As they pass the market on their way, they stop and spend some of their day's earnings on the cheapest available scraps: unpolished rice, rocks of salt, chili peppers, vegetables and fruits out of season. Or pig's intestine or cow's stomach, or even, and this they get for free, fish guts. Soon the cooking fires will start to send smoke up from their chimneys as, one by one, these humble suppers are brought to the boil or fried up.

The sky is turning dark. High up, flocks of buzzards gradually disperse and return to their nests in the forest. The smoke rising from kitchen fires turns from white to soft purple in the rays of the setting sun. From all over the village you can hear the long, drawn out sharp cries of mothers calling their children home for supper.

沈从文
和他的
湘西

祠宗九嵩

When I wander these streets and watch the people go about their daily lives, and observe them celebrate their joys and mourn their misfortunes, I, too, seem to absorb something from them, to understand more of the meaning of life.

I have seen almost too many of those riverside streets. They have taught me so much. The majority of writings were inspired by the scenes and people of those streets. I love these places, these people. Their lives are so pure and simple. So much so, that thinking of them leaves me feeling sad.

. . . . It is impossible not to be touched when

you come across the people, their good and bad sides, the light,

the color, the customs, and the spirit of Xiangxi. Nor is it possible

for a city dweller not to forgive the locals their ignorance, their

sly cunning.

Every Monday and Saturday there is a market for barter and exchange held here. People come from villages up to twenty-five li away to trade. On the days of the market, people start to congregate even before dawn. Just about everything you could imagine is available, and you will find people from all areas and walks of life doing business.

Note: A li is a traditional measure of distance, approximately equivalent to one-third of a mile or half a kilometer.

If you have ever traveled anywhere in the south of China, to the west of Hunan, then you will recognize the sound of the cries and shouts that rise from the marketplace. If you listen from a distance, the rise and fall of the hubbub will bring to mind the image of waves crashing on a shore.

People rush hither and thither, shout and call to each other, gesticulate wildly, and yet in all this indescribable chaos there is some sort of order. Once a deal has been done, the buyer and seller heave sighs of relief, shout with joy—or exasperation, it is hard to tell—and then head off for the tent where they are selling strong liquor. There, over a couple of drinks, the money changes hands.

You could buy anything you wanted at the market: bolts of cloth; beef and mutton; oil; salt; the finest Hunan pastries; red-threaded rope; fake jade bracelets; the three character classic, the *Book of a Hundred Names*. Whatever it was, you could find it here. Then there were people selling dog meat, whole legs of it. And the prices were much cheaper than in Chenzhou. Each of us kids used to buy rock candy for about twenty cash, which we would stick in our mouths and suck on as we wandered around checking out what was going on.

湘西 和他的 沈从文

The people who did business in the marketplace used to shout across at each other, and bargain with each other, with such a rapid fire banter that it seemed as if they were reciting some sort of religious chant, as opposed to speaking any normal language.

. . . . Ah Qin walks from stall to stall in the

market. Today there are many young Miao minority women there.

The style, the sound, the very character of the market is full of

youthful vigor… But you must admit that the young girls of the

Wupo clan are the most seductive and bewitching. Their charms

are more intoxicating and debilitating than the strongest liquor.

Although these designs are still considered thoroughly up-to-date, the fact is that they derive from the Chu Dynasty, over two thousand years ago. The patterns and motifs are just the same as those you would find in an ancient piece of lacquerwork, or on a bronze mirror. Yet still they possess a youthful vitality. They seem to leap for joy, like a local folk dance, and they possess, moreover, a kind of "rhythm," like a dance, too.

沈从文
和他的
湘西

· · · · · · · · · · · · · · · · · Τhe women who sell chickens squat behind the wicker baskets in which they keep both cocks and hens. To them, they are all the same. They are prepared to haggle hard over the tiniest amount of money. Try to drive the price too low and they'll go wild with fury.

He takes his square butcher's knife and slices meat for whoever wants it, however they want it. When he has to cut through a rib or a hard bone though, he will reach for his fine-edged and thick-ridged chopper. Only that will do the job. He stretches out the blade and in a flash it swooshes down and thwacks through the meat and into the block. Immediately after he makes the cut, his shoulders and arms quiver for a moment, just like the meat does.

沈从文 和他的 湘西

Hanging around at the market with nothing in particular to do, you might well run into an older relative who'll ask you, "Have you had anything to eat?" You are both hungry, and after an awkward silence you laugh timidly. He knows the form better than you and says: "Come on! This won't do. How can you come to the market and not buy something to fill your stomach?" And then, as if it was the most natural thing in the world, he'll pull you by the arm to the dog meat stall. There the pair of you buy a jin or two of dog meat which you have chopped into pieces. You pick up a piece, dip it into the salty sauce and pop it into your mouth.

Note: A jin is equivalent to approximately one pound.

Pig's intestine stuffed with glutinous rice, sliced and then lightly fried in oil—it is almost enough to make you swallow your tongue. Then there were Yang Nusan's pig's blood twists. People would come from as far away as their stall over by the East Gate to satisfy their lust for them. One bowl was never enough. And the stall that sold beef cakes never had to solicit for business. Anyone who passed by would have to pinch their nose or else they would suffer an irresistible temptation to stop and buy some.

沈从文和他的湘西

Even if we got ourselves nothing to eat, we were still happy in the market. We wanted for nothing more than to soak up the atmosphere, the mass of undistinguishable smells from all the stalls to hit our noses, the sounds, the colors. We employed all our senses to absorb the taste and flavors of everything—all of our senses that is, without actually using our tongues or putting anything in our mouths.

Shortly before suppertime, the market empties and what was a bustling space becomes just an empty beach. A little later, apart from the dogs fighting over and chewing the leftovers underneath the butchers' stalls, there is no sound other than the sound of punt poles scrunching the riverbed.

沈从文
和他的
湘西

· · · · · · · · · · · · · · · · · · In a word, there is no one who ever had

something to sell or buy who did not go to a marketplace and do

his business, at one time or another. When the time and need arises,

such a place becomes a mayhem of man and beast, a chaos of

commerce, and yet it possesses a spirit that a traveler from afar

cannot fail to be absorbed by and irresistibly drawn into.

沈从文
和他的
湘西

Seas are deep and wide. Waves look like mountains as they approach the shore. Yet the sea is reassuring, comforting.

A river is like a fire. If you get too close to it, any minute it might swallow you up. Yet all it is concerned with is running its own course. What is amazing about a river, though, are the men who live on it and make their living by it. They are incredibly skilled in dicing and dueling with the river and still escaping its clutches.

They rely on the water. They must understand the water. More than anyone else, they need to understand, and respect, the power of the river. Yet every day, every minute of their lives, they have to be prepared to leap from its lethal eddies, to escape its clutches.

Every time a small boat heads for the safety of the shore, it must fight its way through fierce waves and treacherous currents. But at the same time, that boat must always be ready to run from them, too.

CHAPTER SIX

THE BOATMEN

The boatmen are strong and brave, and fine looking. They are excellent singers. They can swim. They can fight. Their language is coarse. As they cast off onto the water, they seem like fish. When they come ashore and go to their women, they behave like wild pigs. By day they handle their boats, by night they play cards and ma jiang. They are as skillful at one as at the other. Although there might be many men to a boat, each knows his place and his duty. There is no disorder. The decks of the boats are always perfectly organized and clean, as if they were brand new.

I guess that those lights and that noise are either coming from the raftsmen enjoying themselves on their rafts or else the boatmen and the local flower girls drinking. Most probably, that girl is wearing a gold plated ring that the boatman brought specially for her in Changde Prefecture. While she sings, she pats down the hair above her temples with the hand that is now wearing it. What a perfect picture. I know, and share, their joys and sorrows. Though they seem so distant, I feel so close to these people as they pass their days, with tears and laughter.

It is impossible to imagine the day when boats could ever do without the grubby tow men on this stretch of river. Nature has put a river here, and on that river it has built banks. The fate of the people who live along those banks has been ordained by nature, too. It is set in stone, as solid as the rocks themselves.

. . . . To pull the freight boats past this place,

the tow men bend double and stretch their bodies as taut as the

tow ropes. As they pull with their hands and push with their legs,

they cry out in unison, "Ah one, and a heave! Ah two, and a

heave!" Slowly, the boats inch upstream.

When the boats go downstream, they can rely on the power of the current. When they want to go upstream, they use another source of natural power: the sturdy and strong tow men, and their hawsers woven from bamboo strips. Yes, those are the men I am talking about. Those strong and honest men of the riverbank. You can find these men, these "things," anywhere, anytime along the river. They are simpler to take care of than a dog. Give them some food to eat and they will work for you from dawn 'til dusk, giving freely their strength and sweat in return.

湘西 和他的 沈从文

. . . . "Come on! Hurry up...Hey mister! Your mother feed you nothing but bean curd? Is that why you are so weak?" The boatmen shout at the tow men until their throats are hoarse. They are egging them on as they crawl along bent double under the ropes. Other than the shuffle of feet along the deck, the only other sound is the boatmen's sighs: "Hell! Come on granddad! Put your back into it!" The fact is that there is no lack of effort on the bank. It is the boat that is not responding.

I make a calculation in my head. The helmsman gets eight fen a day. One jiao and three fen for the bowman. One fen and two li for the deckhands. That is all it costs to get these men to do their share of work from dawn 'til dusk, in all weather. Tell them to jump in the water and push, they jump straight into the water. Tell them to go ashore and pull a rope, they'll do so without question.

Note: A li is a tenth of a cent. A fen is one cent. A jiao is ten cents.

· · · · · · · · · · · · · · · · · · The custom of the river is that boat hands do not get paid on downstream trips. They get fed. We take a simpleton with us who sits at the prow of the boat with an oar in his hands, diligently splashing the water with it. He is blissfully happy and does not cost a cent. When the boat prepares to return back upstream, the boat hands get their pay in advance and buy gifts, such as Daiheji face powder or Dasheng imported cloth. They'll present them to their girls when they get home.

They can be unhappy, when a boat runs aground, when the weather is too hot or too cold, or when the boat charter treats them harshly. But they can be happy, too, and full of laughter, when a strong breeze fills their sail, the food and drink are good, when they are making vulgar jokes about women.

湘西 和他的 沈从文

· · · · · · · · · · · · · · · · · I lie in the opening of the cabin and watch

the boatmen casting their long poles into the rapids and the

rocks, swearing coarsely as they do so. Vulgar as they are though,

I always think of them as pure of heart. As we go to land, the cur-

rent desperately tries to sweep us away. It is too strong. Just when

we think we have gotten through the worst of it and are all but

ashore, a boatman changes his pole from one side

to the other, and in an instant the boat gets snatched away again

by the current and pushed back into midstream.

When the boat makes a voyage, they help pull on the oars and push on the punt poles. These young boat hands are serving their apprenticeship. They must pay close attention to all that happens around them. They need the experience and they need to learn the skills. Not only do they learn how to read the water and the wind, to memorize the position of the rocks, and how to use an oar and pole, they also learn what it is like to get a scolding and a beating. And they listen carefully, too, to the coarse language and colorful oaths that constantly fly about their ears all day long. One day they, too, will use such language to swear at others, and then at their own children.

湘西 和他的 沈从文

············ When a boat's crew disperses at the end of a trip, they will share a rough meal and finish off the odd jobs that need doing. Then, if they have money, they'll gamble and rashly blow it all away. When the boat sets off again everyone hopes for an early landfall so they can fill their bellies with a good meal. Once in a while, under the white moon and in the cool night breeze, they will dream of a happier life. They will forget the burning sun and soaking rain. They sing simple and beautiful songs to drive away the bitterness of their lives.

These people can only speak the coarsest of language, and make liberal use of vulgarity. It seems as if they have also lost all idea of punctuation and grammar. The meaning of their words is easily lost in the shambles of their speech. From father to son, between brothers, they cannot communicate except by this crude language. Yet once they have eaten their pickled cabbage and rotten meat, their dinner conversation as foul as the food, suddenly they will burst into the most beautiful, poetic, and haunting song!

. . . . At daylight, the big rafts of timber cast

off from the shore, and prepare to continue their journey. One

by one, the men who slept ashore come down and join their

mates who stayed on the raft. Together they untie the logs from

their moorings. The sound of stakes being ham-

mered and logs being chopped fills the air.

These men spend their lives in continuous strife and struggle. To them, a "vacation" is an unknown concept. Their backs bared to the blazing sun, they pant and sing. To quench their thirst they drink straight from the river. It does not even cross their minds to pray to Buddha for protection or peace. When the boat pulls up beside a temple, the captain may well go in to burn incense and kowtow, but to the deck hands a temple is purely a place where the wind-cooled stone terrace under the eaves is a good place to catch some sleep.

The men of the river do not begrudge the fact that their lives are spent in endless toil. They give their health and strength willingly. Then, when they grow old, or are struck down with cholera or dysentery, they lie down in an empty boat, or out in the sun, and quietly pass away. Thus their lives run to their end. There must be at least 100,000 men living lives like that on this stretch of river. Thinking of their forbearance and their fortitude, I let out a sigh.

. . . . No one could count up and give you precisely the number of men working on the river. Not even the local official who collects the river dues could come close to getting it right. They live their lives like a postman. Unless there is some exceptional circumstance, when they might spend a stretch of four or five days, or even a half-month or whole month with their families, their days are spent coming and going on the river.

Note: In the rural areas of China in those days, postmen had to spend most of their time delivering mail to remote villages.

As for the boatmen on the Chen River, they love to stop off at "Lü's Place." In fact it is something of a joke to stop off at "Lü Jia Ping." They pretend it is an actual place name. When they go ashore they'll pick a couple of girls and enjoy a little "mouth to mouth." To visit a prostitute in no way contravenes the mores of the river people.

Note: The Chinese character Lü (呂) is made up by two of the characters that mean mouth (口).

湘西 和他的 沈从文

. . . . On every boat you will see women, chil-

dren, and young brides-to-be already living with their future

husband's family. On the one hand, the boatmen do the jobs

allotted to them by the traders who charter their boats, and on

the other they do the work given to them by God, raising

a family. They are competent at both.

very problem, every question, has a simple answer on the river. The conduct of the boatmen is governed by deep-rooted custom. If someone's boat has a head-on collision or someone is unfairly harming someone else's business, there is always a traditional solution to the dispute. And presiding over this traditional justice will be a man of many years and great wisdom.

沈从文
和他的
湘西

Inside, by the light of the stove or a small oil lamp, a cook throws some fish guts into the blackened pot, along with a bunch of chilies. Immediately the pungent smell of hot peppers mixes with the smoke and steam and people in the room sneeze and turn their heads away. After a while, in the semi-darkness, everyone will eat their daily meal, either standing or squatting in the place allotted him by habit or family standing.

"Hey, brother! Uncle! Do you want yellow wine or white liquor?" The man's face lights up; he is in the mood for a joke, and he is getting interested in the girl behind the counter. Pretending to be riled with anger he replies: "Yellow wine? You don't look that young or stupid but still you ask me if I drink yellow wine!" And with that, she takes the bamboo ladle and pours him an earthenware bowl of strong, cold white liquor. She promptly takes it over to his table and places it in front of him.

"Me? Rich? Huh! Why should I lie to you? Deduct my basic cost of seven jiao. The going rate in Tao Yuan is one dollar and a bit. Then there's the running expense of getting there and back, and how on earth am I going to make any money from a shipment of 15 pounds or so, I ask you!" The old boatman went on whining about how unfair it all was. But when he started to talk about the girls on the back canals of Tao Yuan and their special tricks, the whole boat burst into tears of laughter.

Note: A jiao is the equivalent of ten cents.

Once the food is finished, people warm their feet by the fire. Thanks to the daily soaking they get on the boats and from the rain, their feet are puffed up and the skin white. Then the more talkative ones start telling outrageous stories, in incredibly dirty language, both of which they have picked up along the river. Behind the talkers and the listeners the flickering firelight throws up shadows on the wall, which stretch and contract as the flames rise and fall.

· · · · · · · · · · · · · · · · The old man of the river wanders up and down its banks, his bright eyes sparkling, checking out each and every boat that passes. He recognizes just about every boat captain and boat hand from this township and the surrounding area, and hails them as they pass. He jokes with the youngsters, too, either asking them how many fire-breathing dragon boats they have seen on the stretch from Changde or how many bowls of lamb noodles they ate at the Pavilion of the Drunken Immortal. Or else he teases them about how many times they played "Three Corners" in Tao Yuan county, and how many times they screwed around.

Note: By fire-breathing dragon boats, the man means the new steamboats.

Maybe someone will bump into a boatman on the tannery street and will ask him: "Boatman, 'Good water should not be used to irrigate another man's fields.' Why do you let another man make himself at home with your woman, and you then have to spend your hard earned cash on another?" But that boatman will pat the deerskin purse attached to his belt, and reply: "Uncle, 'The wool still comes from the sheep's back.' This money ain't mine, is it now? Where do you think it comes from?"

沈从文 和他的 湘西

"Little Blacky's dad, old Zhang Shun, is waiting for Blacky to get home with his boat. He has a load of tangerines he wants him to take down river! Has he gotten as far as Changde yet?"

"I don't know. You better ask Zhu Mao Mao. I saw him and Blacky in the same batch of boats by Chen Zhou. They moored up together at Shang Nan Men and went off whistling to the Christian church to see Jesus and hear the priest preach." Then, as an afterword: "Jesus loves me when I hollers! And I love all his foreign dollars! Ha ha!"

. . . . That boatman has lost all his money through bad luck at the gambling table. He is just working out how to win it back when an old man disturbs him, and suggests an honest day's work. He bristles with anger and rudely shouts at the old man: "Get lost you old fart! All we care about, us young guys, is women. You want boats? Then go down to the river. You'll find all the damn boats you want!"

· · · · · · · · · · · · · · · · · Fırst he knocks on the door, using the old

boatman's signal. Then he whistles softly. The door opens and he

puts one muddy calf over the threshold. The other muddy leg is

still on the outside when she wraps her arms tightly around him, and

his freshly shaven, yet coarse cheeks, burned by the sun and washed

by the rain, come up close to her soft and warm round face.

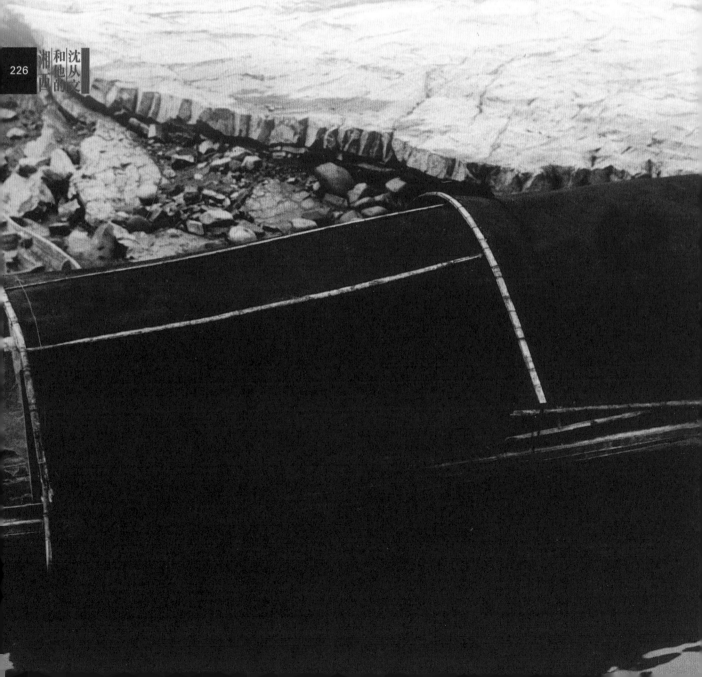

Men crawl from beneath warm quilts, leave their women and stagger down from the stilt houses where they have been lodging, through the rocks on the shore, and back to their boats. The women, prompted by the affections of the night before, go to the windows and shout down to the men "Look after yourself! See you next time!" But it is obvious that both parties are already counting the cost of the one night stand, with tears and resentment.

沈从文
和他的
湘西

· · · · · · · · · · · · · · · · · The memory of his woman's laughter,

the way she moves, is clamped on his heart like a leech. To have

such a woman is worth more than a month's hard work, more

than the wind and rain and fierce sun on the deck of the

boat, more than all the money he lost at cards, more than…

Now is the time to start saving up for his future.

No woman can ever be guilty of a sin. When God created woman, he followed the manual for perfection. First, he made her beautiful. Second, he made her intelligent. Third and finally, he made her fall in love with man. He did not overlook a single thing. And with woman, he completed his task of creation.

When a traveler from afar comes to the ferry jetty, he is in for a surprise. Such a beautiful stretch of water! Such a pretty hillside town! And even more amazing, if he looks closely, just about all the boat hands on the ferries are women!

Once he has crossed on the ferry and disembarks at the opposite bank, enters the town and wanders the streets, he will find that the vegetable and rice sellers, the stall holders, the silversmiths, every single one of them is a woman. There is nowhere else in the world where it is so common and so natural for women to be employed in every job and

CHAPTER SEVEN

THE WOMEN

every trade. If you witness it for yourself though, you will surely wonder: if the women here are taking care of every aspect of daily life, like that mythical country in the book *Jing Hua Yuan*, then are all the men away fighting a war, or are they at home, taking it easy, watching the children?

The women relieve the men of the river of all their cares and worries. They replace them with a contentment and a sense of oblivion that is better than alcohol or opium. Just about every man who works on the river dreams of finding solace with one of these women.

Note: *Jing Hua Yuan (Flowers in the Mirror)* by Li Ruzhen (1763-1830).

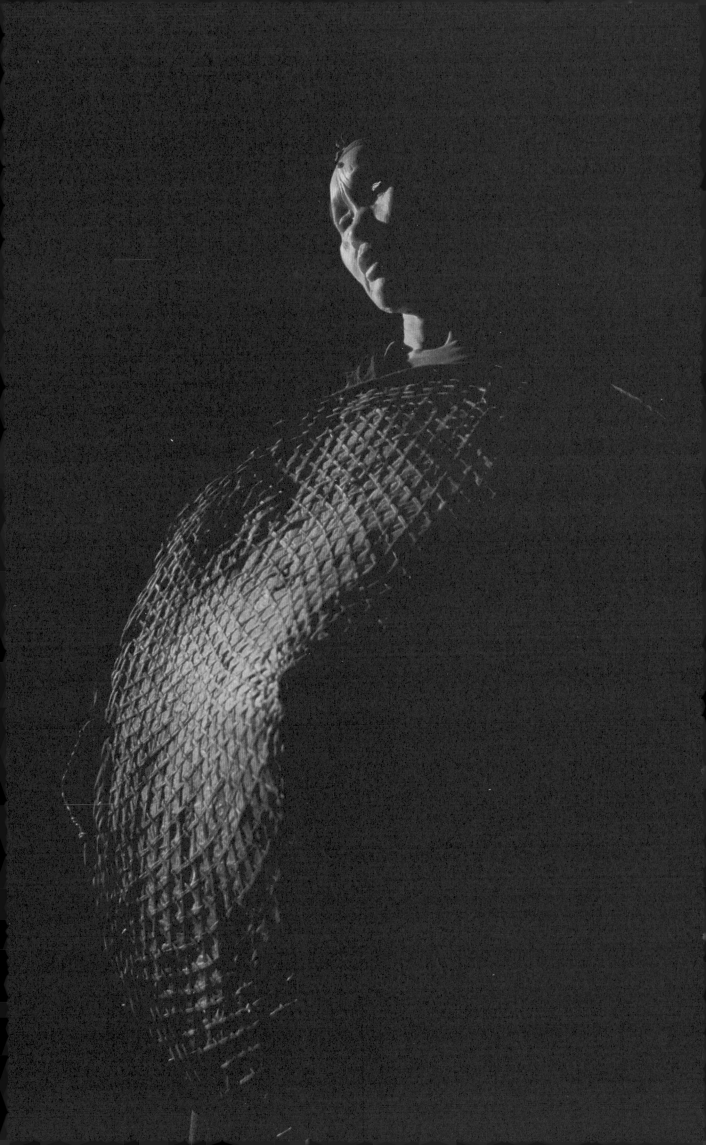

. . . . Each woman of Xiangxi, at some stage in

her life, will end up as a fierce middle-aged spinster, an old witch

or a courtesan, skilled in the art of entertainment as well as the

art of love. The "hysteria" she succumbs to at each of those stages

is one of the secrets of the mystery of Xiangxi. Behind that mys-

tery also lies much tragedy and poetry; her stories, were they

told, would break your heart.

No matter how ordinary or mundane they may seem, the lives of the womenfolk of Xiangxi are full of magic, mystery, and feeling. They believe in the local folk tales that transport them to a beautiful and gentle fairyland, and they believe that heaven and the gods will protect them from calamity.

In the second and eighth months of the lunar calendar, musical recitals are put on to thank the local deities for protecting the village through winter and then bestowing a harvest. Many of the plots of the stories involve beautiful women who martyr themselves for love. And these songs form the basis for the village girls' spiritual education. The narrator of the tale will often speak of "The minister who never served a second lord," "The wife who died rather than remarry," and the like. It might all be fantasy but the girls will live their lives according to those moral tales.

· · · · · · · It is not the custom in the villages to take girls as slaves or handmaids. If a family needs domestic help, the head of the family will invite a girl to become the bride-in-waiting for one of his young sons. The practice is common. Just about every family counts such a girl among its members. And from a practical point of view, it teaches the young prospective couple about life.

When these girls are a mere twelve or thirteen years old, they put on a pair of trousers of imported patterned cloth and proceed to their future husband's threshold. On the way, they pay respect to the village gods' temple with a rooster as a symbolic companion. Then they take on their new identity as a bride-in-waiting, as a member of their future husband's family. They might be young but they will take part in every task in their new household, even the most strenuous. They will go down to the river to wash clothes, tend the fire and cook in the kitchen, and much else besides.

When the future bride is fourteen or fifteen years old, it is expected that she should have begun to understand more of the world. She should begin to develop feelings of affection for her adopted family. She will learn to sew and embroider with her aunts and the neighbors. On her apron, with five colors of silk thread, she creates mandarin ducks frolicking in lotus flowers, or magpies chirping in a plum tree. On her silk shoes she sews a small pair of phoenixes.

She loves to admire a new bride with her heavily powdered face. She loves to listen to stories about newly wedded couples. She loves to stick wild flowers in her hair. And she loves to listen to singing. She already knows how to appreciate the finer melodies of the songs from Cha Dong.

. . . . The most important moment in a young

girl's life is when she becomes a bride, and must leave her mother's

side. Moreover she is about to become someone else's mother.

She has so much to learn and to discover. It must be like a dream

for her. To go and sleep with a strange man in his bed, so as to

carry on his family name. Of course she is frightened. Naturally,

she will want to cry. So, naturally, she does.

The lives of the women of Xiangxi may well seem so remote from the norms of society at large, yet they are also so close in spirit. The way and why they laugh and cry, their joys and sorrows, triumphs and defeats, all are not so far removed from women of another age, another place. Their happiness and sadness suffuse their very existence, turning black to white, and obliterating memories.

沈从文和他的湘西

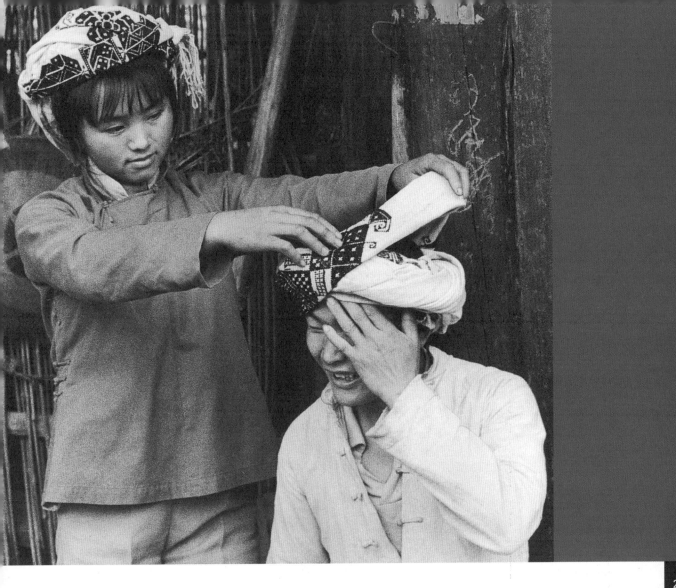

· · · · · · · · · · · · · · · · · · · It is his right hand. As usual, he is gesticu-

lating wildly with it, making rude gestures to the girls. When he

notices someone looking at him, he pulls it back and pretends to

be scratching his ear. Even a world famous artist could not cap-

ture the moment. His actions, what he is thinking right now, not

even a writer could express it clearly. Words simply cannot

describe this character, whether he is good or bad, handsome or

ugly. He is beyond the scope of description and depiction.

If you were to take the softness and gentleness of one of these women and make a trap out of them, a fine net, somewhat like a face veil, no single sinner would ever escape once they had been ensnared by it. No matter how much they boasted that they could. The immortals, who can fly like gods across the clouds and swim through mist like fish, if one of them so much as laid an eye on the barest inch of white ankle of a Xiangxi girl, he would forget his magical arts forever. So how can mere innocent mortals like us, who are always at the beck and call of the wills and wiles of love, ever hope to avoid becoming ensnared in the fine mesh cast by their charms?

· · · · · · · · · · · · · · · · · · To select the love of one's life by sight alone is highly risky. Our eyes can only give us a vague idea of the general rhythm of the poem that is a beautiful woman. To gain a better idea of this "poem" we need to use our hands. Then we will discover that she is not a poem at all, but a collection of essays. And in that collection of miscellaneous mismatched works, there are parts that do not fit together, even words that are quite wrong. The irony is that the mistakes all occur in the most fascinating sentence.

Below the town is a river. Every day, a countless number of women from the town go down with baskets of laundry on their backs to wash clothes there. They squat on the riverbank, and raise their wooden clubs to beat the clothes clean. Others roll up their trouser legs to display their snow-white calves and stand in the fast flowing water to rinse their stretches of cotton yarn. There are some stepping-stones arranged across the river. They stick up out of the water like the back of a centipede.

沈从文
和他的
湘西

· · · · · · · · · · · · · · · · Whenen the boats arrive, the small chil-

dren's imaginations instantly leap on board with the boatmen.

As for the adults, they are more concerned with their shipment of

young chicks, or brace of piglets, or the pair of gold earrings that

they are about to entrust to the boatman before he sets off back

downstream. Has he brought the two bolts of special black cloth

they ordered? Where is the jar of soy sauce? And those special

quality lampshades for the main room—did he get them?

These and other pressing thoughts like them are passing

through the heads of the housewives lined along the

quayside.

A mother in Xiangxi is like a mother anywhere else, except in a Xiangxi way. She sits on the doorstep and looks out over the street, weaving for her man a stiff cloth belt to wrap around his waist. She props the small home loom up against the door jam and stretches out her thin and pallid wrist. Quick as a flash, her agile hand rams the dog bone shuttle against the end of the loom, and thick cotton yarn spins itself onto the wheel. With her free hand she brushes mosquitoes from her child with a palm leaf fan.

 If you were a young girl in your own

household, you had to put your back into the household chores,

but they were not your specific responsibility. It was rather like

doing odd jobs, or studying for a walk-on part in a Beijing opera.

It was not real work. So it was common for a daughter-in-law to

feel that the days were too short, whereas a daughter

felt they were too long.

Under the low eaves of the houses along the street, all the womenfolk have their heads lowered and are concentrating on the work in front of them. They are tired and when they look up you can see the fatigue in their eyes. As they look across at the stall on the opposite side of the street or see a new batch of cotton belts hanging there, they heave a sigh with a strange air of semi-resignation and set to work again.

沈从文 和他的 湘西

The women feed the pigs and raise the ducks. They collect water and plant vegetables. They twist hempen threads and spin raw cotton into yarn. They grind the millstone and hull the rice. There is nothing they cannot do, and nothing they do not do. Working as if they were forced labor, in the burning sun and soaking rain, makes them into strong and healthy women and inures them to hardship. They become physically strong. Thanks to all the locally grown tangerines they eat they also have bright eyes and their blood flows clear and strong. All this makes them good for bearing children.

By local custom, it is better to be a daughter than a daughter-in-law. A daughter-in-law spends her entire day busy with household tasks. If she has not been put to work in the fields, she must feed the pigs and let out the chickens. She must stir the gruel and cut the hay. Then she has to sweep up the ash of the rice straw fuel from beside the stove and use it to bleach the cotton clothes. Next she must go down to the river to wash the vegetables for pickling. She is so busy all day that she has no time to rest.

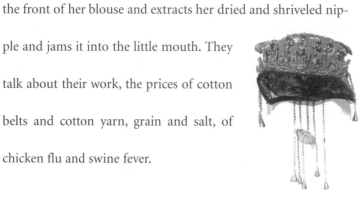

Sometimes the women pause in their work and take a break. With nodding heads they chatter among themselves. A baby cries with hunger so its mother pulls open the front of her blouse and extracts her dried and shriveled nipple and jams it into the little mouth. They talk about their work, the prices of cotton belts and cotton yarn, grain and salt, of chicken flu and swine fever.

沈从文 和他的 湘西

When a young couple is deeply in love, once they have finished kissing and necking, they make a vow that when they are apart they will remain true to each other. For forty or fifty days, both the man sitting on his boat on the river and his wife on the shore will while away the hours staring listlessly into space. Their hearts are tightly bound to each other, despite the distance. The wife will most likely be the most sincere, pining to the point of madness.

No matter how poor and humble their lives, how difficult and tough their work, everyone puts their utmost into making ends meet and making the most of their lot. For sure, there are days of tears and laughter among their joys and sorrows, days of plenty and days of want when it comes to food and drink. As the seasons change, from hot to cold and back again, these people feel those changes far more acutely than anyone else in the world. History means nothing at all to them. But if you were to delve into the past thousand unchanging years of their lives, of which no record exists, or could exist even, you will find a pathetic tale that defies description.

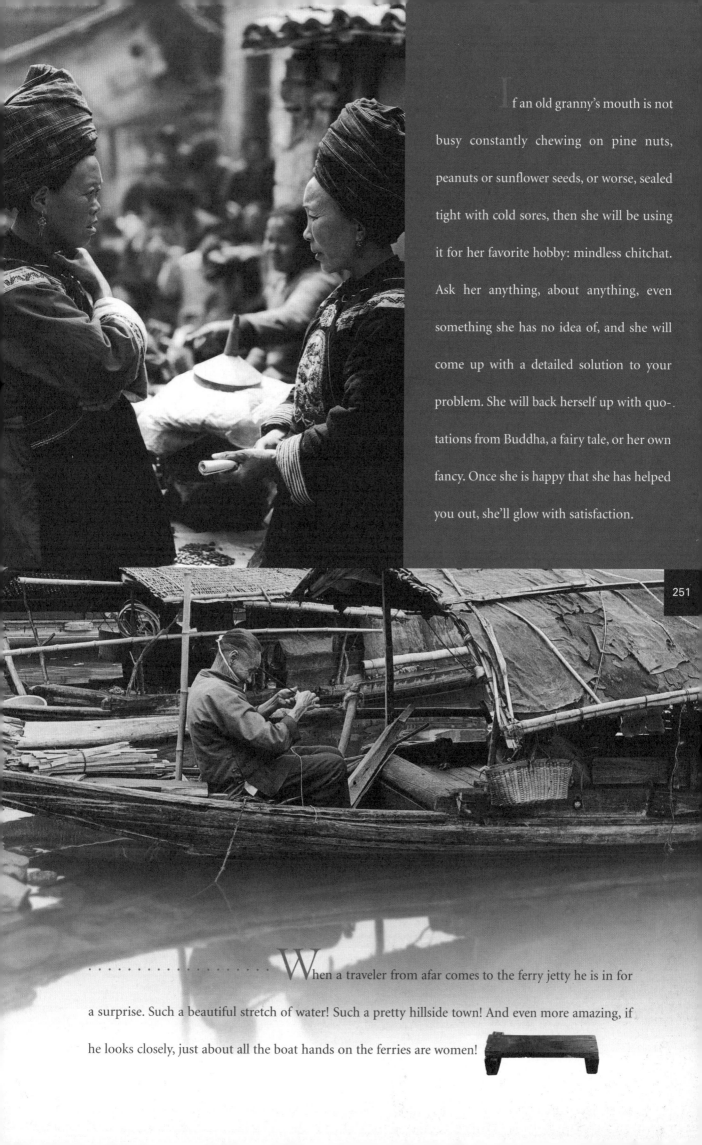

If an old granny's mouth is not busy constantly chewing on pine nuts, peanuts or sunflower seeds, or worse, sealed tight with cold sores, then she will be using it for her favorite hobby: mindless chitchat. Ask her anything, about anything, even something she has no idea of, and she will come up with a detailed solution to your problem. She will back herself up with quo-. tations from Buddha, a fairy tale, or her own fancy. Once she is happy that she has helped you out, she'll glow with satisfaction.

When a traveler from afar comes to the ferry jetty he is in for a surprise. Such a beautiful stretch of water! Such a pretty hillside town! And even more amazing, if he looks closely, just about all the boat hands on the ferries are women!

J ust because they are working hard all day does not mean that these women forget that they are women. And women are born with an urge to make themselves beautiful. They decorate the fastenings on the front of their shifts with patterned cloth, and do the same with the ankles of their trousers. They do this work by the light of the tea oil lamp when they have some spare time at the very end of the day.

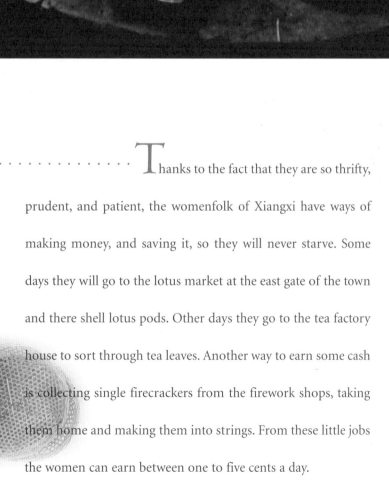

. . . . Thanks to the fact that they are so thrifty,

prudent, and patient, the womenfolk of Xiangxi have ways of

making money, and saving it, so they will never starve. Some

days they will go to the lotus market at the east gate of the town

and there shell lotus pods. Other days they go to the tea factory

house to sort through tea leaves. Another way to earn some cash

is collecting single firecrackers from the firework shops, taking

them home and making them into strings. From these little jobs

the women can earn between one to five cents a day.

"I do not believe you."

"Now why should you not believe me? You young people, you don't believe anything, and you'll never understand anything either! 'It'll be fine for Qing Ming, and rain later in the spring.' You never believed that. And as for: 'The Thunder God never strikes someone who is eating'…You never believed that either, did you?" The old woman is exactly like any other you can find all over China. Her head is full of nothing but old wives' tales and maxims. Such sayings made up a major part of her education.

Note: Literally: 'If Qing Ming is fine, Gu Yu will rain'. Qing Ming is the day for the grave sweeping festival and marks the beginning of the fifth solar term, April 4 or 5. Gu Yu (the Grain Rains) falls on April 20 to 22, the time to sow the fields.

In spring the days grow longer. As the sun increases in intensity, the old folk of the town either sit outside to warm themselves in its rays or slip inside for a nap. Youngsters with nothing better to do fly kites from the grain drying ground or anywhere else where there is enough space. The hot sun moves so slowly across the sky. The clouds seem more sluggish too and give little respite from the heat.

      · · · · · · · · · · · · · · · · "Who knows the names of those diseases they have in towns. As far as I know, those town folk love to get sick. That's why they have lots more names for illnesses than we have. How on earth could we knock off work just because we got some bug or other? We just got malaria, fever and dysentery. We don't need none of those fancy illnesses in the country, no we don't."

The old woman bought a chicken for

seventy cents. At first she thought of telling everyone it cost

eighty cents and pocketing the difference. But Mrs. Yang explod-

ed when she tried this, and Mrs. Gui got on her case, too, so she

started babbling excuses like a string of sutras. "How could I get

one any cheaper than one dollar? You don't believe me? Go ask

for yourselves! Finding a bundle of useless feathers like this was

harder than finding a needle in a haystack! You want such a pre-

cious chicken, then you try to find one for less than a dollar. No

way was anyone going to sell it for ten cents less! You get me a

ten cent coin in change for this and I'll bloody well jam it

between my two front teeth!"

湘西 和他的 沈从文

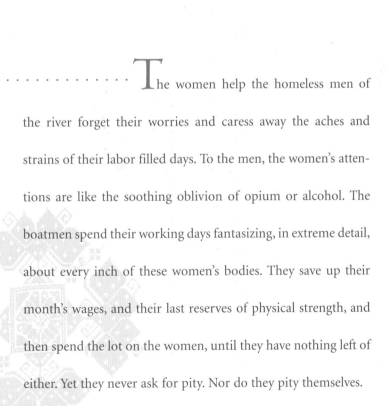

The women help the homeless men of the river forget their worries and caress away the aches and strains of their labor filled days. To the men, the women's attentions are like the soothing oblivion of opium or alcohol. The boatmen spend their working days fantasizing, in extreme detail, about every inch of these women's bodies. They save up their month's wages, and their last reserves of physical strength, and then spend the lot on the women, until they have nothing left of either. Yet they never ask for pity. Nor do they pity themselves.

If there is anything different about the people of Xiangxi, it is that they are more straightforward and direct, and therefore more casual. The men and women enjoy short-term relationships, marry and settle down, or else simply take a one-night stand. To them there is no moral distinction or difference to whichever way you choose to enjoy the comforts of a woman's charms. They do not find loose behavior obscene or shameful. Observers of their way of life should not adopt the self-righteousness or moral rectitide of a scholar, or belittle the natives' simple ways of looking at life.

The background and roots of the women of Xiangxi are similar to those of Qiao Xiu. The reason why lies somewhere in the wild spirit of their youth and the gentle madness of their later years, the guileless warmth and the welcome they give to strangers, the way they break the rules of local customs. To borrow a waterborne analogy: "You must never give up until you reach the Yellow River." But these women are like the fresh mountain streams of Xiangxi, which never reach the waters of Dong Ting Lake. They linger in these small towns, they stop over at the piers along the river bank, and pass the rest of their days here.

On a sunny day when there is nothing to do, the women sit at the gate of their homes, making shoes and embroidering the toes of them with a pair of phoenixes in fine green and red silk. Or else they make a patterned purse for their lover who is away upriver. They watch the passersby and fritter away the long day. Others might lean on the windowsill overlooking the river and watch the boatmen unloading, listening to them sing as they climb the masts. When evening falls, they take turns in catering to the traveling merchants and the boat hands. Their ministrations include all the tricks and arts of an accomplished courtesan.

"Old woman, I really can't believe that you cut quite such a figure in your day."

"You don't believe me do you? Well then, first let me take an oath that what I say is true. Then let me tell you young man, about how all those rich men used to chase me. So many of them I can't even remember. But there is one, an official, I remember well. I can picture him now; how he took off his own finely embroidered silk belt and wrapped it around me. How he used to light a candle for me. I swear on my life that I am not making up a single word!"

沈从文
和他的
湘西

. . . . Although life has its small ups and

down, when it comes to the final reckoning of the major dis-

putes, the serious grievances, then there can be only winners and

losers. When you sum it all up, the lives of these people are

closely related to nature. They devote their lives, and their wits,

to living in harmony with it, and at times fighting with it.

Just like all inanimate objects in the world, they converge and

disperse, bloom and then fade away through

the seasons of life.

沈从文

和他的

湘西

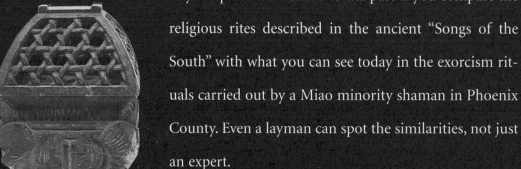

During the period of the Warring States, the great poet Qu Yuan was banished from the state of Chu and made his way here by small boat. As you travel here yourself, you will see the mountain scenery he describes, and the fairy spirits he invokes in his poems, come to life—just as you will smell the rotting manure and the fragrant flowers that inspired his pen. Likewise, you will discover how closely the present is related to the past if you compare the religious rites described in the ancient "Songs of the South" with what you can see today in the exorcism rituals carried out by a Miao minority shaman in Phoenix County. Even a layman can spot the similarities, not just an expert.

I often dream of my days as a soldier, sitting in a small boat, playing cards, telling coarse jokes. I love to, like the characters in the story *Hui Ming*, take a big square basket to the river to rinse the rice in it. And I am happiest when I can take up my pen and paint a picture of the typical people of the country. Like the perverted old Taoist priest in *The Priest and His Temple*. My friends' bosses

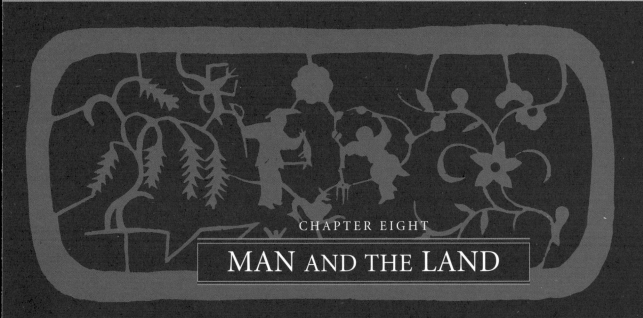

CHAPTER EIGHT

MAN AND THE LAND

were all like the characters in the story *Enlistment*. My stories like *Long Mi* and *The Vegetable Garden* give the best idea of what my life was like in those days, my joys and sorrows.

. . . . It makes me sad and a little lonely, this return of spring. From the darkness that covers the river, you can just, only just, make out the merry songs of the men pulling their oars. A trader's boat in the very middle of the stream is looking for a place to moor. The sounds of song float across the water. When I hear the words, they give me a profound sense of revelation. At last, in a flash as it were, I understand the words: "It is no use to flick through the pages of history, let alone study it." Who does not feel heartbroken when they face up to history?

· · · · · · · I used to be an out-and-out country bump-kin. Then I went on my travels through Sichuan, Guizhou, Hunan and Hubei provinces. I covered twenty-eight counties and much ground. Of what I learned, much had to do with human nature, and of that much was really very straightforward. A young person of today's world who has been born and brought up in a town would find that very hard to comprehend.

沈从文
和他的
湘西

. . . . In an area that traverses from south to north the mountain range that borders the county of N, there are some fortified villages, at the base of the mountain slopes. In them live the remnants of a people that history has forgotten, that time has passed by. They speak another language and follow different customs. They even have different dreams. For many years now they have lived on the edge of society, at the farthest reaches of the modern world.

They live by the will of heaven. Their lives and all that goes on in them are governed by fate. Each lives his own life and raises his own children. Should they have hopes or resentments they go to the nearest temple and air them to the priests or gods. Once the gods have settled their troubled hearts, they return home to live on in peace and tranquility.

Each of the seasons—spring, summer, autumn, and winter—brings its own regrets and yet also brings hope and happiness. And those joys and regrets bring tears to people's eyes. Just before the year's end, a Miao shaman, in all his finery, will be invited to the house to beat his gong and drum and seek redemption from the gods for the keeping of the year's vows, and beseech wealth and happiness from them.

The old prison warder is adding up his life's savings. He has trouble working it out exactly. Every month he has earned twelve strings of cash. He has put aside some of it every month for the past five years of his working life. He has decided which one of his adopted sons will take care of the money, and he has chosen his own grave clothes and coffin.  Everything is in order. But he cannot help wondering, as he reminisces, why did he never get himself a wife?

Some people are waiting for the fine to be paid by their family. There are others who wait for the announcement of their execution by the Yamen. As each of them waits, they are all confused by the turn events have taken. They can only watch the sun's shadow creep up the wall, wait for the dusk to creep into each corner of their room or cell. They eat a little of the prison gruel that they are given. When there is a disturbance in the jail, they are taken out and made to lie prone on the rough–hewn stone of the building's forecourt. Their trousers are pulled down to reveal their grubby buttocks, and they are given thirty or forty strokes of the cane.

The counsel to the Yamen must possess the skill to tell fortunes, or he will not be taken on as an advisor. To be a military advisor, one must at least have a skill that is part heaven-sent and in part developed through practice. It seems that all three men come from Chenzhou. When you see the counsel making his Taoist incantations, you will be convinced that he is a reincarnation of Zhuge Liang.

Note: Zhuge Liang was a legendary state advisor in the period of the Three Kingdoms (AD 220–265) and is a symbol for resourcefulness and wisdom.

· · · · · · · · · · · · · · · · · This good old fellow loves to tell stories

of ten years ago, of his glory days. Every now and then he gets so

wrapped up in his own stories that he will throw in some harm-

less bragging. For example, if he saw the Provincial Governor

Cai E two times, then before you know it he

will have told you it was five times. And then

he will forget he has said it, even if his listener has not, and thus

he will claim he is innocent of ever having made the boast.

· · · · · · · · · · · · · · · · Ah Ya died young and probably all she

left was the fairy tale about the bamboo flute. (May her soul rest

in peace!) Ever since then, I have always thought that

the flute was the best instrument for accompanying

the Buddhists' and Taoists' ceremonies. At funerals, for

example, when you cannot get yourself to cry, a few notes

on the flute gets the tear ducts gushing like nothing else.

Their lives prove how life can be so rich, full and varied even when it exists in conditions of base ignorance and abject poverty. When an intellectual comes into contact with these people, and their lives, he should be ashamed if he cannot at least empathize with them. For an intellectual to genuinely understand how solemn and sincere these people are is almost impossible.

散度姜节

. . . . . . Even farther away, you can hear the sound of the skin drums and the copper gongs. That means the people of a distant village are marking the end of this year's co-operation between man and nature. They must have had a bountiful harvest and are holding a ceremony in the fields to thank the gods and the local spirits. What's more they will be entreating the gods for "more of the same" next year.

I face a row of rocky crags topped by a line of trees. A tall solitary tree clings onto a cliff. A pavilion stands by a bridge. Small hills and gullies form a backdrop. Whenever I see these masterpieces of nature, I can only stop and revel in them. I am often amazed that the audacity of nature can produce an effect so vastly superior to the ingenuity of man.

. . . . I t seems as if all sorts of plants and flowers are competing for space to grow. Under the warm rays of the sun they fulfill their allotted task. Peacefully they stand in the rows where they have been planted by nature's unseen hand. They sprout leaves and burst into flower. But once they have flowered, their life's work is still not complete. Beneath the shade of their leaves, at the base of the plants, tiny fruit is gradually taking shape.

An even more serene and remote place was the rooftop ridge of that small pavilion. Because it was so high it was perfect for looking far out over the countryside. And at just about any time of day there would be small birds, whose names I never knew, singing from the top. Some of them seem so utterly content, lost in their own song. They sang with elation at just being alive. Others seemed to be extremely agitated, as if they were urgently seeking a mate. Their impatience was the epitome of a lifelong yearning for love.

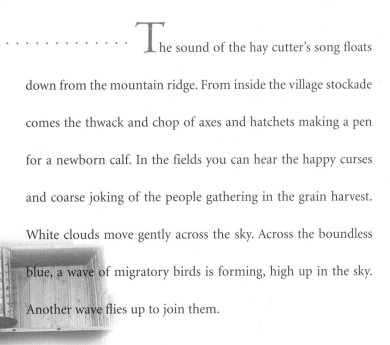The sound of the hay cutter's song floats

down from the mountain ridge. From inside the village stockade

comes the thwack and chop of axes and hatchets making a pen

for a newborn calf. In the fields you can hear the happy curses

and coarse joking of the people gathering in the grain harvest.

White clouds move gently across the sky. Across the boundless

blue, a wave of migratory birds is forming, high up in the sky.

Another wave flies up to join them.

After the Mid-autumn festival, the whole countryside looks resplendent with nature's wealth. The farmer's year of labor has come to an end. The fields are scattered with golden haystacks and temporary storehouses made of fresh cut white wood. The whole land looks like an oriental tapestry. Up behind the back of the village, the mountain range is covered in the luxuriant green of the trees. The China firs tower up to the sky. From a distance they look like a sea of deep black green.

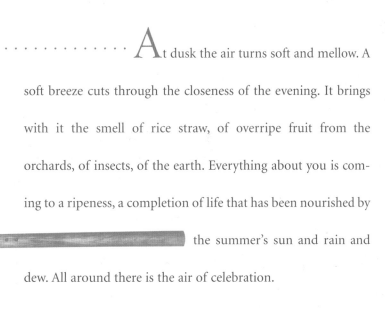

. . . . At dusk the air turns soft and mellow. A

soft breeze cuts through the closeness of the evening. It brings

with it the smell of rice straw, of overripe fruit from the

orchards, of insects, of the earth. Everything about you is com-

ing to a ripeness, a completion of life that has been nourished by

the summer's sun and rain and

dew. All around there is the air of celebration.

If you look up at the village from down in the threshing ground, the stockades and animal pens seem to form a castle wall around the houses. The mass of trees above swells over the rooftops like a protective shelter. The village looks like a thriving metropolis. Then cast your eyes down at the countless fields that cover the hillsides and fill the gullies. They look like a pile of steamed cakes.

· · · · · · · · · · · · · · · · · The rice seedlings have already been harvested from the fields that line the small paths through the paddy. Only short white stumps are left where the plants were a few days ago. The straw from the rice is stacked up here and there, like a hamlet of small houses. All around, there is the persistent yet intermittent sound of insects chirping, like a small orchestra playing a plaintive autumn nocturne.

There are people who love to hear the sound of oars splashing in the water. There are others who think the sound of wind and rain is beautiful. There are even some simple-minded folk who find music in the sound of a baby crying or hear words in the whistling of the reeds in a breeze. All of those sounds are like poetry. Yet even more beautiful, something that can really send you into a stupor, a daze, is the voice of a pretty pale-faced Miao girl singing her song.

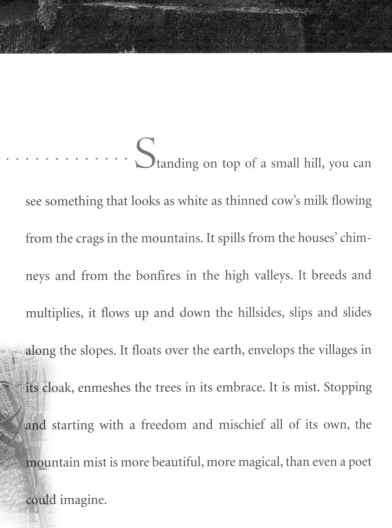

. . . . Standing on top of a small hill, you can

see something that looks as white as thinned cow's milk flowing

from the crags in the mountains. It spills from the houses' chim-

neys and from the bonfires in the high valleys. It breeds and

multiplies, it flows up and down the hillsides, slips and slides

along the slopes. It floats over the earth, envelops the villages in

its cloak, enmeshes the trees in its embrace. It is mist. Stopping

and starting with a freedom and mischief all of its own, the

mountain mist is more beautiful, more magical, than even a poet

could imagine.

No matter how happy and joyous this bright and beautiful scenery makes you, there is still, lying latent, deep within it, a sense of desolation and sadness. Although all around is life, activity, there is still an overwhelming sense of calm. The autumns of a thousand years ago were more than likely exactly the same as they are today. And in each and every one there will have been the same sadness, the same loneliness, as I feel today.

In my life I have visited many strange places. I have crossed every shape and size of bridge. I have sat in all sorts of boats. I have slept on every kind of bed. But I have never experienced an evening such as that of a couple of weeks ago, when I stretched out on the finely carved big nanmu bed in the country mansion of the Man family. The cries of the mountain birds, near and far, the hiss of the kettle boiling over in the kitchen— all those sounds ripped my heart from my chest and sent it soaring into space.

The snow is melting. From the ditches all around the fields, the thaw is running into the small streams. Just like a river rushing toward the sea, the tiny rivulets babble with joy and anticipation. From the bamboo groves where the snow still lies thin upon the ground beside the same streams, the cries of the wild birds compete with the budding shoots of plants to announce the arrival of spring. Nature is plucking at my heartstrings.

This old monk is wearing a short robe. A fine pair of eyebrows traverses his broad forehead. He might be old, but his spirit is still full of vigor. He is just like the kind of monk you read about in novels who has found the "Way." When he sees that two men both have knives he asks them: "Are you from the ninth clan?" The older of the two replies with respect, "Yes. We belong to the Zong generation." "Then you must be Mr. So-and-so's son?" "Yes, I'm sorry to say that we two useless fools ain't considered worthy to bear the name Wu of the ninth clan."

Because of this place's history, no one dares live here. But because so many boats have to pass by, several decades ago a temple was built. Thanks to the temple, the crews on the boats that traveled through the night past this scary place feel reassured and safe. The temple is above the riverbank, on a hill-top. An old monk lives there alone. But because the hill is so bleak and desolate, very few people climb it to light incense before the Buddha.

The violet turtledove, with his bright and beautiful neck, stands in the snow. He is already summoning his friends with his cooing. I want to admire the soft lilac light of the morning sun on the snow on the roofs of the village houses. Like houses where there has just been a wedding, they look half in chaos, half so calm. Outside of the dwellings, the rising sun blesses with beauty the snow-covered landscape, the tiny streams, the wintry woods, the white hills. Along the banks beside the roads, a solitary hare or crow has left its tracks in the snow, as if painting the proof of its existence onto the master-piece that is nature.

沈从文
和他的
湘西

. . . . T here is not a single color that does not appear in the clouds. It is as if there is a magician somewhere in the heavens, who is forever moving them from place to place and altering their shape and hue. Now that the sky has been washed clear by a recent rain shower, the view is filled with a freshness and energy like that of a person who has just recovered from a long illness.

When this wind brushes against you, it feels so refreshing, and yet also wearying. It brings on an indefinable melancholy. Its touch is like a grandmother's hand softly stroking your cheek, or a mother's fingers running through your hair, tugging gently at your collar. With it comes the many varied scents of flowers and the smell of wood, hay, and leaves. There is also the pungent whiff of the earth on it.

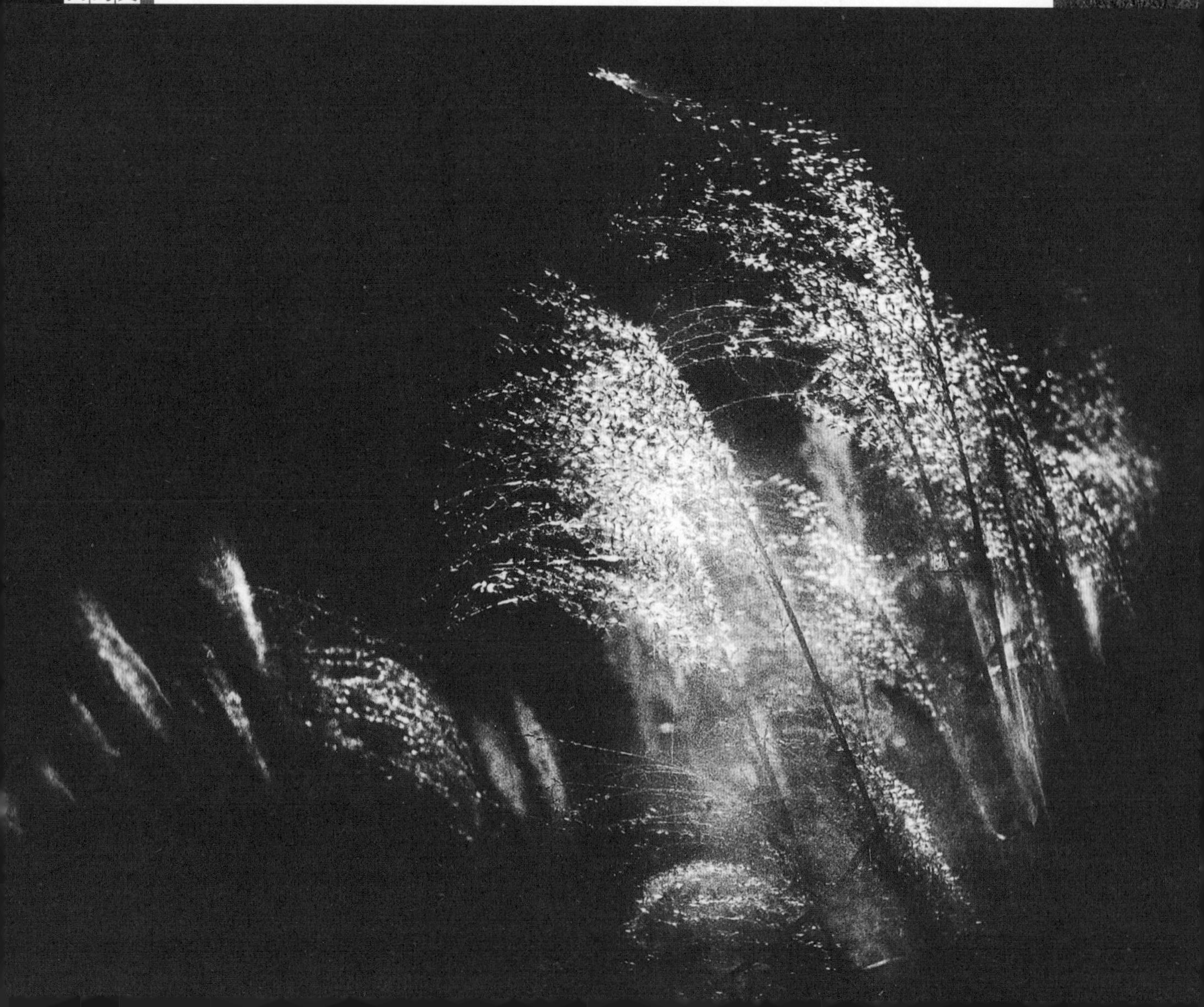

沈从文
和他的
湘西

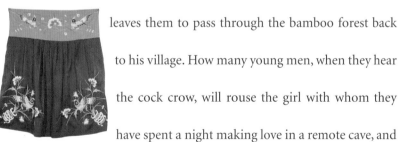

The dew seems to soak into the night cries of the crickets. Even the starlight seems softened by its moisture. The weather is too perfect. At this time of year, who knows how many young girls are softly singing as their lover leaves them to pass through the bamboo forest back to his village. How many young men, when they hear the cock crow, will rouse the girl with whom they have spent a night making love in a remote cave, and take her back to her house? How many tears will flow, how many oaths of fidelity will be sworn when the lovers part?

沈从文
和他的
湘西

Now the wind has died away. The wooden clapper of the monk can no longer be heard echoing across the mountainside. Although the calls of the birds in the distance and the closer clamor of the insects along the riverbank might never cease, that does not mean that the world is awake. At times like this, just as with a dream or a piece of magic, it is only possible to clearly grasp, to understand, a fleeting fragment of the complexity of life.

"What use is a family to a thing of beauty? A shooting star, a falling flower, a firefly, the mother hen of the western paradise with her blue head, red beak and green wings, who can sing like no other bird… none of them have a "family." Who ever saw someone raise a phoenix? Who could ever catch a moonbeam?"

沈从文 和他的 湘西

. . . . The lives of the people of Xiangxi, and

their attitude to that life, are very different from those of town

folk, and thus much closer to nature. Nature is poetry. It is a

painting. It stands out so bright and clear, and yet look at it

closely and one can only be struck by how utterly preposterous

 it is! Was the world and all in it really created

by God? Or did mankind invent God? But we

are hardly living in a heaven, or hell for that matter. So life must

be taking place in some sort of abstract plane of existence.

. . . . And so when I took up my pen to describe this place and all that makes it so special, my soul trembled with excitement, and also writhed in agony. I believe that the landscape is so beautiful that any ordinary man, with a willingness to work hard, a comparable zeal and a love for art and beauty could find, among the rich fruit that has fallen from this tree, a seed that gives boundless hope for the future.

In the end I have come to this conclusion:

"Go ahead. Travel even farther afield, to the ends of the earth even. Stake your life on it, place your bet. See if you can pay your way. If we leave our lives to fate, will fate do a better job than us, or make a complete mess of them…?"